I0156744

GAZA:

WHERE HOPE REFUSES SILENCE

Author: Otilia Nicoleta Florea

1 CONTENTS

COPYRIGHT © 2025 by Otilia Nicoleta Florea
ALL RIGHTS RESERVED.
No part of this book may be reproduced or transmitted in any form by any means, electronic or mechanical, including photocopying and recording, or by any information storage and retrieval system, except as may be expressly permitted in writing from the author.

1.1 PREFACE

This book is an attempt to hold together history, economics, politics, and the human stories behind the headlines about Gaza. It draws on reports from international organisations, reputable journalism, and humanitarian actors, and combines analysis with human vignettes to make a complex story feel human and immediate. The goal is not to settle debate but to explain the causes of conflict, reveal the scale of human suffering, and honour the resilience of people whose lives have been repeatedly upended.

Gaza is one of the oldest continuously inhabited places on earth, and one of the most misunderstood. Over the centuries, empires have come and gone, borders have shifted, and yet life has endured on this narrow strip of land by the Mediterranean. Today, that same endurance defines its people — teachers who keep classrooms open under bombardment, mothers who ration light and water with care, and young couples who fall in love amid ruins. Their stories, real and representative, form the heart of this book.

The chapters that follow weave together documented facts and lived experiences. They move from Gaza's ancient foundations to its modern blockades, from markets and schools to hospitals and homes. Some sections draw on verified testimonies and field reports from UN agencies, NGOs, and independent journalists; others reflect reconstructed moments based on recurring realities witnessed across decades of conflict. Every scene aims to remind readers that behind statistics stand human lives — individual, fragile, and infinitely dignified.

This work is written not as politics, but as witness. The intention is to humanise what headlines often abstract, to listen where the world grows tired of listening, and to preserve memory where memory itself is under siege.

Readers who wish to act can do so by supporting credible humanitarian organisations, advocating for policies that protect civilians, and by staying informed through independent, verified sources. Above all, to read with empathy is already an act of resistance against forgetting.

Gaza endures — layered with history, scarred by conflict, yet alive with voices that refuse silence. This book is for them.

1.2 CHAPTER 1 – A LAND OF LAYERS: GAZA'S LONG HISTORY

"Every stone remembers."
— Inscription on an old wall near Gaza City, 1920s

Part 1 — Origins and Early Civilizations

Before the bombs and the border fences, before politics and checkpoints, Gaza was a strip of land kissed by the sea and carved by time. A slender forty-one kilometres along the Mediterranean, it has always been a meeting point — where continents, caravans, and cultures crossed paths.

Archaeologists believe Gaza is one of the oldest continuously inhabited cities in the world, with over 5,000 years of uninterrupted life layered beneath its soil. In the days when pharaohs ruled the Nile, trading caravans from Arabia and Africa rested here on their way to the ports of the Levant. Camels knelt in the sand under canopies of date palms; merchants bartered copper, silk, incense, and grain. The name "Azzah," meaning *the strong one*, was first found on clay tablets dating to the 15th century BCE.

Every empire that passed through left behind more than ruins — they left language, recipes, architecture, and belief. The Philistines built their fortified towns here; the Persians paved roads; Alexander the Great marched through on his way to Egypt. The Romans called it *Gaza Maior* — Greater Gaza — a key stop on the trade route between Asia and Africa. Its port thrived with olive oil, wine, and spices. Later came Byzantine churches, Islamic mosques, and Ottoman markets with arched courtyards and mosaic fountains.

But Gaza was never just a marketplace of goods. It was a crossroads of faiths and tongues — a place where the call to prayer, the church bell, and the sound of Torah recitations once coexisted in the same coastal breeze. Ancient synagogues and early Christian churches still sleep beneath modern streets, reminders of a time when Gaza's diversity was its heartbeat. The stones themselves hold memory; dig anywhere and the past will speak.

Part 2 — The British and the Borders

The twentieth century brought storms no wall could hold back. After World War I, Gaza became part of the British Mandate of Palestine — a decision made not by the people of the region, but by men in faraway rooms in London and Paris. Maps were redrawn like wounds across familiar ground.

Under the British, new borders promised stability but delivered division. Tensions grew as promises to Arabs and Jews collided, and the future of the land was traded between powers like currency. By the time the British withdrew in 1948, the land had already been divided in hearts and on paper.

When the State of Israel was declared, war followed immediately. Tens of thousands of Palestinians — farmers, teachers, shopkeepers, children — fled or were driven from their homes. Many walked for days until they reached Gaza, clutching keys, documents, and photographs of houses they might never see again.

The narrow strip, once a modest coastal province, became a refuge for the displaced. Tents lined the sand dunes; wells ran dry under the weight of so many new arrivals. By the end of that year, Gaza's population had tripled. The United Nations set up relief camps, and people told themselves they were temporary. But tents turned into huts, huts into houses, and what began as exile hardened into permanence. Gaza became both sanctuary and prison — a geography of grief and endurance.

Through the 1950s and 1960s, Gaza lived suspended between two powers and two wars — a narrow strip of longing and resilience caught between history's tides.

After the 1948 Nakba, 200,000 refugees crowded into the Strip — a tiny, wind-battered coast barely forty kilometres long. They came from villages that no longer existed on any map: al-Majdal, Beit Daras, Jaffa, and hundreds more. Their tents, first pitched in sand, became walls of mud, and then concrete. By the mid-1950s, those makeshift camps — Jabalia, Khan Younis, Rafah, Beach Camp — had become small, living cities of their own, stitched together by survival.

Under Egyptian administration, Gaza was governed by military rule. Borders were sealed, movement restricted, and economic opportunity scarce. The Strip became both a refuge and a prison — an inheritance of impermanence. Yet within that narrow confinement, daily life persisted with astonishing discipline.

Mothers baked bread on clay taboun stoves, the dough puffing golden in the smoke of olive wood. Fishermen walked barefoot to the sea before dawn, carrying the smell of diesel and salt. In crowded markets, vendors called out the prices of lentils, thyme, and oranges from Deir al-Balah — the sweet "city of dates."

Children played football with plastic bottles in alleys where British armoured trucks had once rolled, their laughter rising above the static of old radios tuned to Cairo and Beirut. Evenings were marked by the low hum of generators and the distant melody of Umm Kulthum echoing through open windows.

It was a life defined by waiting — for work, for open borders, for the world's attention — but also by rhythm. Fridays brought prayer and rest; weddings spilled into the streets with drums and jasmine; Eid brought sweets baked in borrowed ovens, shared from one refugee family to another.

People adapted the way the sea does: by returning, again, to its own shape. The markets reopened after every raid. The schools, often little more than tents, filled with children learning lessons under the flutter of UNRWA flags. Women washed laundry in basins behind barbed fences. Men repaired nets with hands roughened by salt and history.

In those years, Gaza was a land of contradictions — isolated but alive, wounded but proud. The 1956 Suez Crisis brought invasion and massacre to Khan Younis and Rafah, where hundreds were killed in days. Yet even then, mourning gave way to rebuilding, and rebuilding to routine.

By 1967, when Israel occupied Gaza after the Six-Day War, checkpoints replaced watchtowers, and new currencies replaced old ones. But in the alleys of the camps, life continued as it always had — on borrowed light, borrowed space, borrowed hope.

Despite the occupation, Gaza adapted by enduring. Its strength was never loud. It was quiet, patient — like a candle relit every time the wind blew it out.

Thus, successive generations understood that residing in periods between conflicts nonetheless constitutes living. That resilience is not an act of defiance but of daily repetition — the bread baked, the net mended, the prayer whispered against the sound of distant planes.

Part 4 — The Seeds of Struggle

The First Intifada of 1987 did not begin in a meeting hall or from a declaration. It began on a dusty street in Jabalia Camp

— with the screech of tires, the crack of metal, and the shattering cry that followed.

An Israeli military truck collided with a line of Palestinian workers returning home from Israel. Four young men were killed instantly. Their bodies, wrapped in flags and carried through the camp, became the spark for what decades of occupation and humiliation had already prepared: a generation too weary to remain silent. By the next dawn, the city was alive with unrest.

Boys who had grown up drawing the sea on school notebooks now filled their hands with stones. The sound of chanting rose from alleys — voices raw and trembling with anger and faith. "Freedom! Dignity! Palestine!" Women banged pots from balconies in solidarity. Mosques broadcast not just the call to prayer, but the call to stand. What began as mourning became movement.

The uprising spread like wind through olive groves and across the camp walls, from Jabalia to Rafah, from Gaza to the West Bank. It was a rebellion born not from ideology but from exhaustion — from years of curfews, demolished homes, and humiliation at checkpoints.

Israel responded with curfews, arrests, and live fire. More than a thousand Palestinians were killed in the first year alone. Yet for every strike, the resistance found new life. Leaflets printed by candlelight passed from hand to hand.

Children who once counted marbles now counted soldiers. Graffiti became the new literature of defiance — the walls themselves turned into pages of protest. "Here we live. Here we will stay."

In the courtyards, mothers hid their sons under mattresses when soldiers raided at night. Fathers built barricades of old refrigerators and stones. Teenage girls carried first aid in school bags and memorized the names of the wounded. The young learned to live between anger and hope — their hearts hardening, their imaginations still somehow tender.

In Gaza, rebellion and routine coexisted. Markets still opened in the mornings, though shelves were half empty. The sea still shimmered at sunset, even as gunboats patrolled the horizon. The smell of jasmine still drifted through the camps at night.

Resistance became woven into the ordinary. The people learned to carry revolution the way they carried bread — daily, necessary, sacred.

When the Oslo Accords were signed in the 1990s, there was a pause — a fragile, flickering hope. Flags waved. Doves were painted on the walls beside bullet holes. But the reality that followed was far from peace. Checkpoints multiplied, settlements expanded, and the promise of autonomy shrank behind concrete and barbed wire.

Then, in 2005, Israel unilaterally withdrew its soldiers and settlers from Gaza after four decades of occupation. Trucks carried away the last military posts; bulldozers flattened the remains of settlements. The world called it disengagement. In Gaza, people danced in the streets — fireworks, drums, tears. For a moment, the air felt lighter, as if the city could finally exhale. Fishermen returned to the shore with new nets. Children painted doves on the walls.

The borders soon closed tighter than ever. The blockade began in 2007 after the political fracture between Fatah and Hamas, turning Gaza into what the UN would later call "an open-air prison." By 2010, electricity cuts lasted eighteen hours a day. By 2014, three wars had scarred the same ground. By 2020, the UN reported that 97 percent of Gaza's water was unfit for drinking.

The skies that once carried kites and migrating birds became corridors of surveillance — buzzing, mechanical, omnipresent.

Freedom had not come. Only a new kind of confinement — invisible but absolute. And yet, beneath it all, the same spirit that fuelled the first uprising endured.

Children still painted keys on walls for homes they had never seen. Farmers still planted olive trees beside rubble. Mothers still prepared tea for sons returning from protest lines.

Gaza's rebellion was not just in its streets, but in its insistence on life itself — in every birth, every prayer, every loaf of bread baked while the world turned away. Because here, even in siege, the seeds of struggle are also the seeds of survival.

Part 5 — Through Her Eyes — Layla's Story

Layla was born in Gaza City in 1992, in a hospital lit by candlelight and powered by a failing generator that groaned between flickers. Nurses moved through the narrow corridors with kerosene lamps, their shadows trembling against peeling walls. Her mother would later say she came into the world during a blackout — a small light born into a city learning to live without it.

Outside, the Mediterranean exhaled against the shore, and Gaza — fragile, crowded, enduring — carried on. The First Intifada had only just quieted, leaving walls scrawled with slogans and streets heavy with silence. Hope was thin but present — like the faint glow that remains after the candles burn out.

Layla's childhood unfolded in a small apartment above a bakery in al-Rimal, where mornings smelled of sesame bread and diesel. Her grandmother, who had fled Jaffa in 1948, was the family's storyteller. Every evening, she sat by the window, her silver hair pinned neatly, and told tales of orange groves so fragrant the bees would lose their way home. "We lived by the sea," she would say, "and the sea was free — a path, not a border." She spoke of boats that once crossed to Haifa and families that shared bread with neighbours of all faiths. Her voice turned the past into a place alive enough to visit. Layla's grandmother often told the story of that time: how people would hide their grief beneath song, because singing made the pain bearable. "If we don't sing," she would say, "we will forget the sound of our own voices."

Layla's father, a history teacher, believed in facts more than dreams. He taught at a nearby school where windows rattled during air raids and chalk dust mixed with concrete powder. At home, his lessons were quieter — about endurance, about the dignity of silence. He rarely spoke of the checkpoints he crossed each morning, where soldiers inspected his books as though knowledge itself were contraband. Nor did he talk of the years he had spent working abroad in the Gulf, sending home the money that kept the roof standing. In their home, silence was not distance; it was protection — a shelter built from restraint.

Her mother, Amal, filled that silence with movement. She kneaded bread, washed laundry in rainwater, and kept small plants alive in chipped cups on the balcony. "If something grows," she used to say, "then we still belong." Amal taught Layla that resistance could be quiet — that caring for the insignificant things was its own kind of defiance.

By the time Layla turned sixteen, Gaza was a city enclosed by walls and waiting rooms. The blockade, imposed in 2007, had already begun to shape daily life — electricity rationed to a few hours a day, water arriving in trickles, and shelves half-empty. Still, her parents insisted on keeping her in school. "Education," her father said, "is the only gate they cannot close."

That same year, she met Omar — a tall, soft-spoken engineering student who carried blueprints instead of notebooks. His hands were always smudged with graphite; his eyes carried a light that looked east, beyond the fences. They met by chance in a library crowded with students studying by candlelight. She was reading Mahmoud Darwish; he was sketching bridges.

He smiled at her book and said, "Bridges are like poems — they connect what others say is impossible." Layla laughed. "In Gaza, even metaphors need permits." But he kept talking — about tensile strength, design, connection — and somehow, between equations and verses, she found herself listening to more than his words. Omar spoke of bridges that would connect Gaza to the world, not only with steel, but with the will to live. "One day," he told her, "I'll build one that carries us across."

Their friendship became a secret rhythm between sirens. They met during short hours of electricity, traded letters wrapped inside borrowed books, and lingered after class as the muezzin's call rolled through the dusty air. When the power failed, their conversations continued by phone until batteries died. Their love grew like jasmine through concrete — unseen, persistent, fragrant.

Then the war of 2008–2009 began. Omar's university — the one he loved like a second home — was bombed on the third day. Classrooms collapsed; the engineering lab burned. He returned after the ceasefire to find his professor's notes buried under dust. Instead of leaving, he gathered a few children from the neighbourhood and began teaching among the ruins, using broken doors as desks. "If the walls fall," he told his students, "We will learn on the ground."

Layla joined a women's literacy centre downtown, where cracked windows let in dust and sunlight in equal measure. She taught young girls to read their names — the first act of reclaiming identity. She also wrote small poems and essays for underground newsletters that travelled on USB drives smuggled through the border. "Words are lighter than cement," she wrote once, "but they build stronger walls."

Their love became a quiet act of rebellion — not loud or dramatic but enduring. When the city went dark, she lit a candle on the roof and whispered a prayer for Omar's safety. When the curfew lifted, he brought her a single white stone from the ruins of his campus. "So, we remember what can rise again," he said.

Letters passed between them, carried in the most ordinary ways — slipped between loaves of bread, folded into textbooks, hidden in shipments of notebooks bound for schools. Sometimes weeks passed before she heard from him. But the letters always came.

In one note, Layla wrote, "When I can't find you, I talk to the sea. It answers with waves that sound like your name." Omar's reply came days later, written in ink so faint she could barely read it: "Then I will speak to the wind, so it can carry my voice back to you." She kept that letter folded inside a small tin box beneath her bed, alongside her grandmother's house key from Jaffa and a bundle of dried jasmine petals. During the long blackouts when the city dissolved into silence, she would take it out, trace the words with her fingers, and whisper to herself, "We are still here."

Because for Layla, love was not a luxury — it was survival. It was the courage to dream amid rubble, to believe in bridges that could not yet be built, to write as if the world might still be listening. And through her eyes, Gaza was never only a tragedy. It was a living thing — scarred, luminous, defiant. A place where hearts learned to rebuild faster than buildings, and where even in the darkest nights, something green — or human — always dared to grow.

1.3   CHAPTER 2 – THE SIEGE OF SURVIVAL

"To live here is to measure time by the sound of drones and the silence that follows."
— Testimony from a Gaza teacher, UNRWA report, 2019.

Part 1 — The Wall and the World

By 2007, the sea had become a mirror of confinement. After Hamas took control of the Gaza Strip, Israel and Egypt imposed a blockade that sealed more than borders — it sealed futures. Overnight, a territory already crowded became a cage. Every bag of cement, every lightbulb, every medical scanner, even crayons and notebooks for children, had to pass through a web of permissions, inspections, and prohibitions.

Before the blockade, Gaza's markets brimmed with colour and noise: oranges from the orchards of Deir al-Balah, fish from the blue waters off Gaza City, spices and fabrics from the Sinai and Hebron. The air carried the scent of cardamom and roasted coffee. Families strolled the seaside promenade at dusk, watching fishing boats return with their catch.

Now, shelves stood half-empty. Prices doubled. Power cuts came like clockwork, slicing the day into intervals of light and dark. The hum of generators replaced the buzz of conversation. On some nights, the only illumination came from candles and the blue glow of mobile phones — small stars flickering inside crowded apartments.

The blockade was justified by its architects as a matter of security. But for two million people inside the Strip, it became a slow, invisible suffocation. Hospitals ran on aging generators that coughed and sputtered in the night. Farmers watched their crops rot when exports were banned. Fishers were shot at for crossing invisible lines in the sea.

An elderly man summed it up for a visiting journalist: "We are not living — we are waiting. Waiting for permission to exist."

Part 2 — A City of Shadows

Layla's family lived on the third floor of a building with cracked walls and water dripping from the ceiling. Each winter, the rains leaked through bullet-pocked concrete, tracing slow silver lines down the walls. The smell of damp plaster mixed with the faint sweetness of kerosene lamps. When storms came, the wind slipped through broken window frames, humming like an old ghost that never left.

The power came for four hours a day, sometimes less. When the electricity arrived, the city came alive in a flurry of urgency — washing machines spinning, stoves lighting, laughter spilling out of windows. And when it vanished again, Gaza sank into a low hum of generators, the air heavy with diesel and dust.

When the fridge went silent, Layla and her mother packed food into metal bowls, lowering them into buckets of freezing water on the balcony. They prayed it would last until morning. In the apartments nearby, neighbours did the same. Every act of survival echoed through the building — water carried in reused jugs, candles placed in glass cups, whispers of gratitude and fatigue.

Omar had found work with a small NGO, documenting damaged schools and clinics. His notebooks filled with names, numbers, and brief stories — how many windows broken, how many classrooms roofless, how many children still attending. "Sometimes," he told Layla, "I feel like we're writing the city's obituary before it dies."

Yet even amid the silence of failure, Gaza refused to stop breathing. Children still walked to school past rubble, balancing backpacks, and laughter. Street vendors called out prices under tarpaulins patched with plastic. Families gathered around flickering lanterns, sharing what little food they had. The scent of baking bread and coffee drifted through the narrow alleys, proof that life, however bruised, would not yield.

Unemployment rose above 50%, among the highest in the world. Young men stood idle at street corners, diplomas folded neatly in their pockets like forgotten promises. But women — resilient, inventive — carried the city forward. They baked bread in home ovens, stitched dresses by candlelight, and tutored children for a few shekels an hour.

Ingenuity became its own quiet rebellion. Layla often said, "If the door is closed, we'll make a window." And somehow, they always did — not out of glass, but out of will.

Even in a city of shadows, people found their own light.

Part 3 — The Sound of the Sky

In 2014, war returned to Gaza.

It was not sudden — everyone had felt it coming, the way the air thickens before a storm.

It was the longest and deadliest assault since the blockade began. For fifty days, the sky itself became a language of fear. The United Nations reported that more than 18,000 homes were destroyed, and half a million people displaced — families moving not by choice but by survival, carrying mattresses, prayer rugs, and photographs down roads lined with rubble.

Every explosion had its own signature. Some began as a hum, a low metallic whine that grew into a thunderclap; others struck without warning, swallowing whole streets in a single breath. The horizon flashed white, then red, then the kind of black that swallows sound.

Layla's neighbourhood was hit on a heavy August night, when the air was so hot that windows were left half open to catch a breath of sea breeze. The hum came first — that unmistakable vibration that made the ground pulse. Then, without pause, the sky cracked open.

Glass shattered inward. Walls convulsed. The world tilted. Layla grabbed her parents' hands and ran toward the stairwell. Her mother's prayer beads snapped, scattering across the floor like falling rain. The air filled with the smell of burning metal, dust, and fear. When the noise subsided, there was a silence so deep it rang in her ears.

They stepped outside. The bakery below their apartment — the one whose smell of bread had filled the mornings — was gone. In its place was a smoking crater. The awning fluttered in ribbons of flame. Flour and ash coated everything like snowfall.

A small boy, barefoot, was digging through the debris, searching for his toy car. His mother stood nearby, her face-streaked grey with soot, calling his name as if it might bring the building back.

That night, the city's horizon glowed orange from a hundred fires. From the beach to Jabalia, the sound of drones merged with the crack of shelling, a relentless heartbeat in the sky. People didn't sleep; they counted seconds between blasts. The lucky ones prayed. The unlucky became prayers themselves.

Omar's NGO, which had once documented schools and clinics, now became a lifeline. They set up tents for displaced families near Khan Younis, the fields turned into camps overnight. He worked eighteen-hour days, printing names on aid lists by candlelight. Every page became a ledger of the lost.

He met mothers clutching photographs instead of blankets, their children's faces pressed against their palms. He met old men carrying keys to houses that no longer existed, the metal worn smooth by decades of memory. One woman refused to let go of a potted jasmine plant she had carried from the ruins of her home. "It still smells like before," she told him softly.

At night, the camps buzzed with murmured prayers, babies' cries, and the rustle of nylon tents trembling in the wind. Smoke hung low over the horizon like a second, darker sky.

When Omar finally found Layla, days later, she was sitting in the sand beside a torn tent, her dress grey with dust, her hair matted from wind and smoke. Around her, families huddled beneath plastic sheets. Children lined up for bread, their faces pale with hunger and disbelief.

He called her name once, and she turned — her eyes wide, her expression halfway between disbelief and relief. For a moment, the chaos disappeared.

"You found me," she whispered, her voice breaking like glass.

"I never stopped looking," he said. He knelt beside her, taking her hands. Around them, the world burned — but for a moment, they were still.

The sea was only a few kilometres away, but the air smelled of ash, not salt. Smoke curled into the sunset, tracing ghosts above the ruins. Somewhere, a generator stuttered and died. Amid the destruction, their reunion felt like defiance — a small, shining act of love in a world determined to break them.

That night, as they sat beneath a torn tarp, listening to the drone's hum like wasps above, Omar whispered, "The sky sounds tired." Layla nodded. "So do we. But we're still here." And, in Gaza, that was the bravest sound of all — the sound of the living, refusing to fall silent.

Part 4 — Aid and Anger

Relief eventually arrived — convoys of white UN trucks that rolled through the dust like slow-moving ghosts, their blue insignias catching the sun as if to promise safety. The children ran beside them, waving, shouting for biscuits. Foreign medical workers exited their vans, looking weary and pale, with sweat-soaked gloves covering their arms. But the help, when it came, was never enough.

At Kerem Shalom, the main border crossing, trucks waited for days in a no-man's land of sand and silence. Bureaucracy strangled mercy. Each container required forms, signatures, inspections — and sometimes, permissions that never came. Medicines expired before clearance; food parcels were opened, inspected, and resealed under the watch of armed guards. Flour and rice arrived marked "humanitarian aid — not for sale," though everyone knew the black market would claim part of it before it reached the families who waited.

When the gates opened, the crossings breathed for a few hours — and then closed again, like a heart uncertain whether to keep beating. The world called it relief, but here it felt more like survival rationed by schedule. The World Food Programme distributed parcels that barely lasted a week. The International Red Cross delivered medical kits to hospitals that had no beds. UNRWA schools doubled as shelters, the walls painted with cartoons that tried to disguise the exhaustion beneath.

21

Foreign reporters described Gaza as "the world's largest open-air prison." Their headlines travelled across oceans, accompanied by images of smoke and rubble. But the people inside those photographs were not statistics. They were doctors performing surgery by flashlight, their hands steady even when the power failed mid-operation. They were teachers reopening classrooms without roofs, drawing lessons on walls blackened by soot. They were poets writing verses of love on the backs of ration boxes, because paper had become a luxury.

In the alleys, life went on in fragments. Women queued for water at dawn, balancing yellow jerrycans on their hips. Children sold vegetables from baskets woven out of plastic strips. The call to prayer still rose, even when the minarets leaned.

One old man named Youssef, a retired fisherman, planted mint in a broken teapot and placed it on the windowsill of what was left of his kitchen. When a journalist asked him why, he smiled, showing teeth stained with tea and time. "Because it still grows," he said proudly. "And that means we still are."

Anger was everywhere, but it wore quiet faces. Mothers lined up for food parcels and whispered prayers under their breath. Fathers repaired bicycles from scrap metal so their sons could ride again. The city smelled of cement dust and sea salt — and the faint bitterness of frustration, of waiting for dignity that never came with the aid trucks.

Omar had begun volunteering with local engineers to assess structural damage in schools and hospitals. One afternoon, he guided a group of journalists — Europeans with cameras slung around their necks — through what had once been an elementary school. The floors were cracked, the ceiling peeled open to the sun. Children's drawings clung to the remaining walls — blue skies, birds, a word written in Arabic: Salam — peace.

One of the reporters, a woman with kind eyes, turned to Omar and asked, "What do the people of Gaza need most?" He paused. The dust settled slowly between them. The sound of hammers echoed in the distance — men rebuilding walls that could fall again tomorrow. Then he said quietly, "The world sends us flour and words. But what we need is freedom." The journalist lowered her camera. For a moment, the only sound was the wind moving through shattered windows, carrying his answer out to the sea.

That evening, as Omar returned home, he passed another convoy — headlights stretching down Salah al-Din Street like a slow river of ghosts. On the side of one truck, someone had scrawled in chalk: "Help us live, not just survive." He stopped to read it twice, then walked on — the words echoing in his mind long after the sound of the engines had faded.

Part 5 — Women of the Dust

When disaster strikes, it is often women who rebuild the invisible threads that hold life together. In Gaza, this truth was written into every courtyard, every whispered prayer, every shared meal. While men queued for fuel or work permits beneath the sun, it was the women who reopened kitchens, clinics, and classrooms — not in buildings, but in borrowed spaces: stairwells, tents, and rooftops. They became the engineers of continuity.

Layla volunteered at a small community centre housed in what used to be a stationery shop, its walls lined with cracked plaster and handmade posters. There, she taught computer literacy to teenage girls, their faces lit by the glow of second-hand laptops powered by a single solar panel. The hum of the generator outside was constant, a reminder that even electricity had to be fought for.

"If we can't get past borders," she told them, "We'll find a way online instead."

Her students — daughters of teachers, tailors, and fishermen — learned to code in JavaScript, to write English emails, to design posters for small home businesses. They shared one Wi-Fi router that blinked like a heartbeat in the corner. Sometimes, when the connection failed, they wrote their lessons by hand and recited them like verses of endurance.

One girl, Hanan, dreamed of becoming a software engineer. She had never left Gaza, but she spoke of Tokyo and Toronto as if she had walked their streets. "If the world won't come to Gaza," she said, grinning, "we'll send Gaza to the world."

At night, when the city darkened under the hum of drones, Layla stood by the window and wrote in her diary by candlelight. The flame trembled with every passing wind. "Hope," she wrote, "is not the absence of fear; it is the decision to live anyway." Her handwriting was small and careful — a teacher's script — as if steady letters could keep the chaos outside from leaking in.

The literacy rate among Gaza's women exceeded 95 percent, one of the highest in the Arab world, yet employment remained among the lowest. For every university diploma, there were ten closed doors. Still, women refused to wait. They formed cooperatives that baked bread, embroidered dresses, and sold online to markets in Amman, Istanbul, and London.

Fatima, a widow from Shuja'iyya, became known as the Soup Lady. Each evening, she cooked lentil soup for a dozen families, ladling it into recycled bottles. "We feed each other," she said, "so we don't forget who we are."

Others turned their balconies into micro-businesses: one sewing uniforms for schools, another making candles during power cuts, another running an online tutoring service for children in Rafah. When aid ran out, they made do; when hope ran thin, they stitched it back together with thread and faith.

Fatima often said, "We are the quiet army. We fight with soup, with stories, with strength." And it was true. These women didn't march or shout; their revolution was domestic and deliberate — carried out with ladles, laptops, and lullabies.

They became the hidden architecture of Gaza's survival — the invisible scaffolding beneath every rebuilt wall and every whispered prayer. When the men spoke of reconstruction, they talked about concrete and steel. When the women spoke of it, they meant warmth, dignity, and tomorrow.

Part 6 — Corruption, Fatigue, and Faith

Years of siege did not only create scarcity — they created a shadow economy that thrived in the cracks of desperation. Every necessity had a price, every signature a gatekeeper. Permits became currency; connections replaced justice. A single phone call could decide who crossed the border, who received medical treatment, who rebuilt their home first.

At border offices, men waited in lines that stretched for blocks, clutching stacks of papers yellowed by heat and time. Some whispered names of officials under their breath, hoping influence might replace luck. A father might sell his wedding ring for a fuel voucher; a mother might trade gold earrings to secure antibiotics for her child.

Bribes bought travel documents, sacks of flour, extra litres of diesel, or a faster place in the queue when aid arrived. Those who had nothing to offer waited the longest. Bureaucracy became another siege — one that required not courage, but endurance.

On flickering television screens, politicians argued endlessly, their words full of promises that never crossed checkpoints. In cafés with no electricity, people listened to battery-powered radios and shook their heads in quiet disbelief. "They debate," Omar once said, "while we ration candles." Yet even amid the exhaustion, Gaza's faith did not falter. When everything else collapsed — institutions, roofs, trust — belief remained a structure no bomb could touch.

At dawn, the call to prayer rose from the minarets, echoing over the ruins, pure and unwavering. In the old quarter, a few blocks away, church bells chimed on feast days, their sounds mingling in the morning air. Muslims and Christians alike walked through dust-coated streets carrying bread, candles, and blessings.

Weddings were still held, even if the gowns were borrowed and the gold rings fake. The halls were lit by car batteries, the music played from cracked speakers. But the laughter was real — full, defiant, unstoppable. "Joy," Layla once said, "is our most dangerous rebellion."

In hospitals running on generators, babies were born between blackouts, their cries cutting through the low hum of failing machines. Nurses fanned them with cardboard when the air conditioners failed. Outside, fathers paced the corridors, holding small bundles of dates and whispered prayers.

One evening, Omar met an old fisherman mending his nets by the harbour. The man's hands were calloused and dark, his eyes bleached pale from sun and sea. Omar asked why he still sailed, even when the patrol boats fired warning shots near the shore. The fisherman laughed, showing teeth like weathered stones. "Because the sea still belongs to God," he said. "Not to them."

Faith — in God, in love, in tomorrow — was the only currency that inflation could not touch, the only wealth that blockade could not steal. In Gaza, belief was not an escape. It was a discipline — the daily practice of standing up, rebuilding, and beginning again.

Part 7 — The New Generation

A new generation was growing up inside the blockade — their lives measured not by years but by wars. They could list the dates of bombardments the way others list birthdays: 2008, 2012, 2014, 2021. Their childhood memories were catalogued by sirens and ceasefires, by the sound of generators replacing lullabies and the rhythm of survival marking the passage of time. They learned to count not by seasons but by power cuts; to hope not for abundance, but for a few steady hours of light. Their ambitions were modest yet radiant — to study abroad, to find work that could outlast a border closure, to see Jerusalem not through a flickering television screen but with their own eyes.

Among them was Layla, whose life seemed woven from both dust and light. She embodied the quiet, enduring strength of Gaza itself — fragile in circumstance yet unbreakable in spirit. Born in 1992, "in a hospital lit by candlelight," she came into the world during a blackout — a small, breathing flame amid darkness. Her first lullaby was the whine of a generator, her first scent the smoke of kerosene lamps. She grew up above a bakery in al-Rimal, where mornings were thick with the aroma of sesame bread and diesel, and evenings carried her grandmother's stories — tales of Jaffa's vanished orange groves and a sea once free of fences. Her father, a history teacher, taught her dignity the way others teach prayer — quietly, insistently, every day.

As she matured, Layla's spirit gathered layers of grace and intellect. She became a teacher, a storyteller, an advocate for women's education. Her defiance was soft but steadfast — she resisted not through rage but through nurture, through lessons, through the belief that to keep learning was to remain alive. She wrote poems by candlelight and tended small plants in chipped cups, saying, "If something grows, then we still belong." Every act — lighting a lamp during blackout, smoothing a child's hair in a classroom without a roof — became her signature of hope.

If Layla was the heart of Gaza, Omar was its hands. He was a tall, soft-spoken engineering student whose palms bore the callouses of work and the imagination of a dreamer. His notebooks were filled with blueprints of bridges — not just of steel and concrete, but of connection. "Bridges are like poems," he told Layla once. "They join what others call impossible." Where she was intuitive, he was methodical; where she nurtured memory, he constructed meaning. Both shared a belief that love, work, and truth are acts of resistance.

When war reduced his university to rubble, Omar did not stop building. He gathered children from the neighbourhood and taught them geometry and hope among the ruins, using broken doors as desks. Later, he joined humanitarian engineers documenting the damage to schools and hospitals, turning his precision into a language of testimony. His compassion had architecture, his hope had design. In a city that tore itself down daily, Omar kept sketching ways to rebuild.

Their love began quietly — two kindred souls who recognized in each other the same ache to create, to heal, to endure. It grew like jasmine through concrete — fragile yet relentless. Omar's love was not grandiose but constant, revealed in gestures small and sacred: a letter folded into a borrowed book, a pebble offered from the ruins with the words, "So we remember what can rise again." To Layla, every moment with him felt like prayer — not for deliverance, but for the strength to keep loving amid ruin.

They married in the spring of 2008, on the rooftop of Omar's family's building in Shuja'iyya, beneath the faint hum of drones. Strings of battery-powered fairy lights swayed in the wind, and borrowed chairs lined the roof like witnesses. Their vows were whispered rather than spoken:

"To love, even when the world is cruel."

The guests clapped softly, cautious not to draw the sky's attention. When the power failed, someone lit candles inside glass jars. The night warmed — laughter rippling between curfews, drums, and prayers. Against the backdrop of fear, joy bloomed stubbornly.

After the wedding, they moved into a small apartment on the second floor of Omar's uncle's building — a concrete block patched with scars from older wars. The walls were spider-webbed with fine cracks, the windows trembled each time the wind changed direction, but it was theirs. They painted the rooms sky-blue — "to remember the sea," Omar said — though the ocean, only three kilometres away, was often unreachable behind military closures. From the market in al-Zawiya, they bought second-hand furniture: a table with mismatched legs, a dented fridge imported from Italy years ago, doors salvaged from bombed homes. Layla hung lace curtains sewn from her mother's old fabric, softening the daylight that rarely came. When electricity returned, the small fan in the corner buzzed like a fragile heartbeat. For four hours a day, their home glowed.

In late 2009, their daughter Mariam was born at Al-Shifa Hospital. The lights flickered throughout the delivery, nurses moving by the glow of mobile phones, the generator trembling beneath the floor. Medicine was scarce, yet Mariam arrived healthy — a small miracle wrapped in white cloth. Layla sang to her in the half-dark: "Sleep, my sea bird. One day, the tide will open." Omar would sit by the window, his eyes tracing the faint glimmer of Israeli watchtowers along the border. "She was born in a cage," he murmured once, "but we'll teach her how to fly anyway."

Their relationship was never idealized; it was tested by war, grief, and want — yet each hardship deepened their bond. Love, for them, did not escape but endurance — a refusal to let violence define intimacy. When the city burned, they made a world of tenderness from its ashes: rooftop weddings lit by batteries, lullabies between air raids, nights spent counting stars instead of bombs. In their small blue apartment, amid rationed water and endless waiting, they built a universe of ordinary miracles — bread rising in tin ovens, laughter echoing through blackouts, a child's cry mingling with the sound of the sea.

The blockade continued, but so did life — stubborn, fragile, luminous.

In the quiet hours between sirens, Gaza still found ways to love — and in Layla and Omar, love found a way to outlast the siege.

1.4   CHAPTER 3 – FRAGMENTS OF HOPE: REBUILDING HEARTS AND HOMES

"We do not build because we are free.
We build because we must live."
— Masonry worker in Gaza, 2018

Part 1 — The Season of Ash and Light

Gaza stands suspended between exhaustion and endurance — between what has been lost and what refuses to die. Aid organizations call it a humanitarian crisis; its people call it home. Every wall carries both a wound and a witness. Every kite lifted above a ruin is an act of defiance, each fluttering thread spelling the same silent sentence: We are still here.

At night, when the hum of drones finally fades, the sea begins again — patient, unjudging, eternal. The waves touch the broken shore as if counting the survivors.

"I have seen empires come and go," the sea seems to whisper. "Still, Gaza breathes."

Because beneath every ruin, there is a heartbeat. And in Gaza, to keep breathing is itself a form of resistance.

The summer of 2014 was a season of smoke and silence. For fifty days, airstrikes and rockets tore through Gaza's narrow spine — from Shuja'iyya to Rafah, from Beit Hanoun to Khuza'a. The United Nations would later report that more than

18,000 homes were destroyed and over half a million people displaced. Families fled with nothing but blankets and birth certificates, crowding into UNRWA schools and hospital corridors, turning classrooms into dormitories and sanctuaries into morgues. Entire families vanished between heartbeats.

On July 16, 2014, the sea shimmered deceptively calm. Four cousins — Ismail, Ahed, Zakaria, and Mohammad Bakr, aged between nine and eleven — chased a football along Gaza's beach near the fishing huts their family had tended for generations. They had no helmets, no flags, only laughter that carried over the waves. At four in the afternoon, a missile fired from an Israeli naval vessel struck a shipping container near them. Frightened, they ran — small silhouettes across the sand, calling each other's names, running toward the rocks that offered no shelter. A second missile followed, hitting them in full view of journalists watching from the balconies of the al-Deira Hotel. When the smoke cleared, the beach was silent but for the cries of fishermen and the echo of sirens.

The image of their small bodies lying on the sand — their football still rolling toward the sea — travelled around the world within hours, freezing a moment too unbearable to forget. Reporters wept; cameras clicked in disbelief. The Israeli military later claimed the area was a "legitimate target," saying they mistook the boys for militants. No charges were filed. Human-rights groups called it a violation of every law meant to protect the innocent, but the people of Gaza needed no inquiry to understand what they had seen. The Bakr cousins became symbols of a cruel truth: in Gaza, even play is perilous, and childhood itself is an act of courage.

Hospitals ran on fumes. Surgeons at Al-Shifa operated by the light of mobile phones, using vinegar as disinfectant, sewing wounds without anaesthetic. The wards smelled of dust, blood, and diesel — a scent that would follow a generation. Omar, then a young construction worker, joined volunteers clearing rubble in Khuza'a, where bulldozers unearthed bodies days after the bombing stopped. The air was thick with ash and the scrape of metal on concrete. He kept a small notebook in his pocket — a list of names, half-legible, smudged with dust.

"These," he told Layla later, "are not just names. They are the foundations of what we will rebuild."

When the ceasefire came, Gaza was unrecognizable: 2,200 dead, thousands more wounded, hundreds of thousands homeless. Roads had vanished, districts flattened, minarets torn in half. Yet amid the ruin, markets reopened. Fishermen dragged their boats back to shore. Women swept their doorsteps with broken brooms, refusing to let dust become identity.

The morning after the bombing stopped, Gaza exhaled a silence so deep it sounded like grief itself. The air was thick with salt and smoke; sunlight broke through the haze like a shy guest. Layla moved through the shattered alleys, her scarf pulled tight over her mouth. Every step crunched over glass and plaster. Omar walked beside her, carrying their daughter Mariam wrapped in a blanket that still smelled faintly of home. The bakery where they once bought bread was gone; only the twisted metal oven remained. The owner sifted through ashes with a rod, muttering prayers. Around the corner, a woman balanced a tray of tea on her head, pouring for neighbours as if to insist that life, in its smallest rituals, must go on.

And two doors away, a shopkeeper swept his floor. The shelves behind him were almost empty, yet he arranged the few surviving loaves in careful rows. His movements were deliberate — a quiet sermon in defiance.

"This is what Gaza does," Layla thought. "It stands before the dust even settles."

By the next morning, people were already rebuilding. Families stood before the shells of their homes, tracing where walls once rose. Some wept in silence; others picked up shovels, clearing debris with bare hands. Children helped, carrying buckets of rubble, their laughter rising like music against the groan of bulldozers. In Gaza, grief is not stillness — it is motion.

Omar joined a volunteer team organized by the local mosque and UNRWA. They carried clipboards, lists of names, and faith that order could return. Together, they pulled twisted rebar from ruins, stacked bricks, and saved every nail that could be used again. Each fragment became a beginning.

When the first aid convoy arrived, people lined the road — men, women, and children clutching empty bags and plastic jugs. There was no shouting, no pushing, only the slow discipline of survival. A volunteer's voice rose through a megaphone: "One per family!" An old man near the front raised his hand.

"Dignity first," he said. "Always."

At sunset, the muezzin's call to prayer rippled through the haze, echoing off half-fallen walls. Men paused, brushing dust from their faces. Women gathered their children close, whispering thanks for survival. For one golden moment, Gaza stood between ruin and reverence.

Layla looked at Omar — his hands grey with cement dust, his eyes lit by the fading sun — and thought of how the world would call this place broken. Yet here, in the scent of bread baked on open fires, in the laughter of children drawing in the dirt, Gaza still breathed.

It was not the breath of peace, but of persistence — the sound of a city refusing to die.

Part 2 — The Builders of Shadows

In 2014, more than 18,000 homes were reduced to dust in less than two months. The skyline of Gaza — once a jumble of rooftops, satellite dishes, and laundry lines fluttering in the wind — became jagged and skeletal. The city's horizon looked like the cross-section of a wound: open, raw, and stubbornly alive. Yet, even as the air still smelled of smoke and the ruins were warm to the touch, the sound of hammers returned.

Masoud, a fifty-four-year-old mason from Beit Hanoun, went back to work only a week after losing his own home. His hands were thick and scarred, his nails stained with cement that no amount of scrubbing could erase. "If I stop building," he said quietly, "I will start thinking."

Thinking meant remembering — and in Gaza, remembering could break a man faster than war.

He mixed mortar with water fetched from half-collapsed wells, his wheelbarrow creaking over uneven ground. Each block he stacked felt like a prayer — one for his wife, one for his sons still missing under rubble. The sun beat down mercilessly, turning dust into white heat. His face, weathered by salt air and time, glistened with sweat and grief. Still, he worked twelve hours a day, the rhythm of his hammer echoing like a heartbeat across the street.

Cement was scarce — each 50-kilogram bag rationed, tracked, and delayed by layers of paperwork. To rebuild even a single room required approval from multiple offices: Israeli authorities, the Palestinian Authority in Ramallah, international agencies, and local committees. Each demanded signatures, forms, and patience. For many, bureaucracy felt like a second siege — slower, quieter, but equally suffocating.

Masoud and others refused to wait. They collected what the bombs had spared — broken doors, twisted iron rods, shattered tiles. They straightened nails, hammered scrap wood into frames, used plastic sheeting as temporary roofs. One family rebuilt their kitchen wall entirely out of stones gathered from the ruins of their neighbours' house. "They fed us for years," the mother said softly. "Now they shelter us."

In neighbourhoods like Shuja'iyya, Beit Hanoun, and Khuza'a, rebuilding became a communal act — not organized, not funded, but driven by memory and muscle. Men hauled debris with their bare hands, women fetched water from distant taps, and children carried small bricks, treating them like treasures. Laughter and argument mixed with the clatter of tools. The air rang with the thud of hammers, the squeak of pulleys, the scrape of shovels against stone.

"We used to count days by bombs," one resident joked, wiping sweat from his brow. "Now we count them by bricks."

By 2018, the sound of construction had become Gaza's new language — hammers in place of sirens, saws replacing screams. From sunrise to the first evening prayer, the city beat like a living drum. Every rising wall, every patched roof, was not just shelter — it was testimony.

Omar walked through the alleys, his camera slung around his neck, documenting progress. He filmed Masoud's hands as they laid the final stone of a new foundation. The man turned to him and said, "Tell them we are still here. Tell them the dust is building itself again."

That night, Layla wrote in her diary: "We rebuild because we cannot do otherwise. Our grief mixes with cement; our hope dries in the sun. Even in the shadow of ruins, Gaza grows upward." Every repaired wall became a message written in mortar — We are not finished yet.

Part 3 — Love Among Ruins

When Layla and Omar married in 2008, the city was already dusted with ash — and by 2018, nothing had truly changed. The skyline was still jagged, the air still heavy with dust and memory, the streets still scarred by the same wounds now a decade old. Gaza smelled as it always had — of cement and jasmine, of smoke and sea salt, of two worlds colliding but refusing to part. A decade had passed, but time in Gaza did not move forward; it simply circled the same ruins, returning always to loss, and always — impossibly — to life.

Layla's wedding dress was stitched by her cousin from scavenged fabric: ivory cotton rescued from a bombed tailor's shop, lace cut from an old curtain, and a hemline that brushed the cracked tiles like a whisper of what once was. The bouquet was a small bundle of jasmine, tied with a pink ribbon from Mariam's old school project. Every thread and petal held defiance — a promise that even among ruins, beauty would not surrender.

"Why now?" a friend had asked, her voice trembling with both wonder and fear. "Why marry when everything is broken?"

Layla smiled, her eyes glimmering in the candlelight. "Because love," she said softly, "is the only thing they can't bomb."

Their wedding took place in the courtyard of a half-destroyed school. The roof had collapsed months earlier, but someone had strung fairy lights across the broken beams, powered by a car battery that hummed like an exhausted heart. Neighbours brought trays of rice, roasted nuts, and warm bread baked in makeshift ovens. Someone tuned an old radio; the song stuttered through static before bursting into melody, and for a moment even the rubble seemed to sway.

Children danced barefoot, kicking up dust that shimmered in the lantern light. Old women ululated from balconies, their voices rising like echoes of generations that refused silence. A photographer borrowed from an NGO took pictures with a taped-together camera, capturing smiles framed by ruin — proof that joy still found a way to live here.

In Gaza, weddings never stop. They are the pulse of persistence, the heartbeat of a people who refuse to vanish. Couples have wed inside shelters, under tents beside rubble, beneath tarps strung with wire. Each ceremony is both rebellion and resurrection — a declaration that love belongs even in the dust. In Rafah, one bride walked barefoot down an aisle of shattered glass; another posed for photos beside a wall etched with shrapnel scars, her veil fluttering like a flag that would never surrender.

"This is our land," they said. "We want our joy to live here too."

When the power failed during Layla and Omar's vows, no one gasped. Candles flickered to life, lighting faces of friends and neighbours — eyes shining, hands clapping softly, hearts refusing despair. Omar's hands trembled as he slid the ring onto her finger, a simple silver band forged by a jeweller who had lost his shop but not his faith in craft. Their vows were simple:

To love, even when the world is cruel. To build, even when everything falls.

That night, they sat on the roof of Layla's family home. The stars shimmered faintly through the haze, and distant explosions rolled like thunder beyond the horizon. The city exhaled a weary breath — of smoke, sea, and something like hope.

"Do you hear that?" Layla whispered.

"The sky?" Omar asked.

"No," she said. "The city — trying to dream again."

Below them, Gaza glowed dimly — not from electricity, but from candles, lanterns, and the stubborn light of its people.

And ten years later, in 2018, when another young couple married on another rooftop, the scene was nearly identical. The same broken walls, the same borrowed chairs, the same music trembling through static. Children still danced barefoot in the dust; neighbours still brought trays of rice and stories; the same sea still sighed against the shore. Nothing had changed — the blockade, the rubble, the waiting — and yet, somehow, hope remained. Each wedding was not just a union but a declaration that Gaza still loved, still breathed, still dared to dream in the shadow of the impossible.

Because even when the world forgot, Gaza remembered: love does not end in the ashes — it glows within them.

Part 4 — Classrooms Without Walls

At night Layla and Omar watched the city pulse faintly below them, the sound of hammers echoed somewhere in the distance — a reminder that dawn would bring another day of rebuilding. Their candles had barely burned out when the first sound of construction began again at sunrise: shovels scraping against stone, the clang of metal, the murmur of voices calling one another by name.

From the ashes of love came labour, and from the dust of loss came determination.

The first buildings to rise again were schools. In Gaza, education is not only a right — it is the heartbeat of survival. Parents often say, "If the children study, the city breathes again." After every war, the first question asked in any neighbourhood is not "How many are dead?" but "When will the school reopen?"

Omar, still wearing the same worn work boots he'd had for two years, joined a volunteer team rebuilding a primary school on the edge of Khan Younis. There were no real walls — only sheets of UNHCR plastic fluttering between wooden poles, trembling each time the wind passed. The "desks" were old doors salvaged from bombed-out homes, their legs uneven and bound together with wire. The blackboard was a slab of painted plywood, leaning against a wall pitted with bullet holes — a classroom stitched together from the remains of a city still learning how to stand.

When the first day of classes came, more than three hundred children arrived — in uniforms washed by hand, starched with pride, and stitched with hope. Some had holes, some were second-hand, but every collar was straight. They sat cross-legged in the sand, notebooks balanced on their knees, pencils clutched like keys to a door they refused to stop knocking on.

Aya, an eight-year-old with bright brown eyes and a pink hair clip, raised her hand before the teacher even spoke.

"I don't care if there are no walls," she said. "I will learn anyway." Her words rippled through the courtyard like wind through a broken window.

The teachers came without pay, guided by duty more than survival. They carried boxes of chalk and dog-eared textbooks, salvaged from the rubble of another school. One woman wrote the word "future" on the board — the chalk squeaking against the rough surface — and said quietly, "This is what we are rebuilding."

The class repeated the word aloud, their voices overlapping — future, future, future — until it no longer sounded fragile but firm.

Omar stood at the edge of the courtyard, watching the children read aloud beneath the fluttering roof of plastic sheeting. Every time the wind moved, sunlight scattered across their faces. The heat was unbearable by noon, and the roof shimmered like a mirage, but no one left.

Layla visited often, her seven-year-old daughter Mariam skipping beside her, small hands clutching the handles of jugs filled with water and the corners of warm bread wrapped in cloth. The walk to the school was slow, the air thick with dust and the hum of distant generators. When they arrived, Layla would kneel beside the teachers beneath the fluttering sheets of UNHCR plastic, helping the youngest children trace letters in the sand with their fingers. The alphabet shimmered briefly before the wind carried it away, but the children kept writing — again — as if persistence itself were a lesson. Some spelled their names with trembling focus; others etched their hopes into the earth: doctor, pilot, teacher, free. Mariam watched them quietly, her eyes wide with wonder, then joined in — her small hand forming the word home. Layla smiled, her heart tightening at the sight. Even here, amid dust and ruin, words were seeds, and she knew that someday, somehow, they would bloom.

In Gaza, a classroom is not measured by its walls, but by its voices.

Later that week, Omar wrote a message on the side of the school tent with a piece of charcoal: "Built from rubble. Powered by faith."

At dusk, when the call to prayer echoed across the ruins, the children were still there, repeating their lessons under fading light. Their laughter mingled with the sound of hammers rebuilding the city — proof that education was Gaza's rebellion, its resurrection, its quiet anthem against despair.

As Layla watched them pack their notebooks and walk home, the horizon glowed faintly pink — not from fire this time, but from the setting sun. She whispered to Omar, "Maybe this is how peace begins — with pencils." He smiled, brushing dust from her shoulder. "Then let's build more classrooms."

Part 5 — The Network of Help

In Gaza, survival is not an individual act — it is a collective ritual. No one endures alone because endurance here is a shared inheritance. Every home has a story that leaks into another; every heartbreak finds an echo next door.

When a house collapses, five families arrive before the dust settles — carrying blankets, bread, and thermoses of sweet tea. When a child falls sick, neighbours pool medicine, old antibiotics passed hand to hand like heirlooms of hope. When food runs out, meals are multiplied, stretched, and shared — plates moving silently from door to door as though carried by the wind itself.

The city's strength is not built on its buildings, but on this invisible network of human threads, woven tighter each time something breaks.

Layla's neighbour, Fatima, a widow with three children, is part of that web. Her husband was lost during the 2014 bombardment, his body never recovered. She supports her family by sewing dresses from donated fabric, her sewing machine powered by a car battery. One bitter winter, when the sea winds clawed through every crack in Layla's walls, Fatima appeared at her door with a thick wool blanket. "We'll warm each other," she said, her smile lined with exhaustion.

In return, Omar climbed onto her roof the next morning and patched a leak with tar and old plastic sheeting. They exchanged no money, no words of debt — only nods and shared tea. In

Gaza, help is not charity. It is currency, the economy of the heart.

This quiet network of mutual care has always been Gaza's real infrastructure — stronger than concrete, more reliable than any foreign aid. When institutions failed, when borders closed, when the trucks at Kerem Shalom waited weeks to move, people moved for each other.

Women became the city's first responders. In narrow alleys where walls still bore shrapnel scars, they cooked in communal kitchens, stirring lentils in huge metal pots balanced over gas flames. They fed anyone who arrived — neighbours, orphans, strangers. The smell of cumin and garlic drifted through the streets, announcing that someone, somewhere, was still cooking for many.

Shopkeepers in the markets of Shuja'iyya extended credit without keeping ledgers. "Pay me when you can," they said, though most knew repayment would never come. Barbers offered free haircuts to children before Eid. Fishermen brought small catches to families who could no longer afford bread. Each act, however small, stitched another patch in Gaza's frayed fabric.

Omar often said, "This place survives not because of walls, but because of hands." Layla saw it each day in her classroom — students sharing pencils, snacks, even school shoes. When one child dropped out because his father had lost his job, the mothers took turns paying his bus fare. "He is all of ours," Fatima said simply.

Aid agencies like UNRWA, the World Food Programme, and the Red Cross continued to deliver essential supplies — sacks of flour, jerrycans, powdered milk — but it was the people themselves who became their own safety net. What they lacked in resources, they compensated with presence.

At dusk, when the call to prayer echoed through the city, women leaned from balconies passing bread wrapped in newspaper. In courtyards, men gathered to share coffee boiled three times over a single flame. In alleyways, teenagers played music from old radios, turning silence into sound.

Solidarity in Gaza is not an act of generosity; it is a law of survival, a shared moral code that precedes any government or aid convoy. Fatima once told Layla, while ladling soup for a dozen children from the same pot, "We share because it's the only thing that multiplies." Layla smiled. She knew that in Gaza, love itself is communal — it passes from house to house, like light from a candle that refuses to go out. And that light, however fragile, is what holds the city together — louder than speeches, stronger than walls.

Part 6 — The Sea and the Sky

When night finally falls on Gaza, the sea, and the sky merge into one long exhale. The city breathes slower. The generator hum softens, and from balconies lit by candles, the horizon becomes both mirror and memory.

Layla often walks to the shore in those hours — the only place where the blockade feels smaller. The sea, though fenced by gunboats and invisible lines, still moves freely. It refuses captivity. Its waves rise and break against concrete jetties, carrying with them stories from centuries before — Phoenician sailors, Ottoman traders, refugees of 1948, fishermen with calloused hands and salt-stung eyes. Every ripple seems to whisper, we have been here before, and we return.

Omar loves the sea for its labour. Layla loves it for its defiance. Mariam, still young enough to dream without fear, loves it simply because it listens.

They sit together on the breakwater, their feet dangling above the surf. Around them, other families do the same — a nightly ritual that has survived every bombardment. Vendors wheel carts of roasted corn and tea brewed with sage. A group of children chases a half-deflated football, its laughter cutting clean through the air like a hymn.

Beyond the waves, lights shimmer faintly — Israeli patrols, the forbidden horizon. Layla watches them with quiet contemplation. "They think they're watching us," she says softly, "but really, we're the ones who endure." Omar nods, his hands rough from work, his eyes full of both exhaustion and faith.

The sea has always been Gaza's only border that breathes. It carries both hope and hunger. Fishermen, restricted to six nautical miles, cast their nets under constant watch. In 2024, according to the Palestinian Fishermen's Union, over five hundred were detained or shot at sea. Boats were seized; engines dismantled. Yet, each dawn, they return — because the sea, like memory, cannot be surrendered.

Once, Omar helped repair a boat that had been riddled with bullets. Its owner, an old man named Nabil, insisted on repainting it sky blue. "The sea forgives," he said, brushing paint over splintered wood. "It keeps taking from us, but it also keeps us alive."

Layla observed them, hands clasped in silent prayer. "It's like teaching," she said. "We mend what's broken so the next wave can carry us further."

Mariam collects seashells during these visits. She keeps them in a small jar on her desk — white, pink, and grey fragments of survival. When she writes her blog, Echoes of Tomorrow, she sometimes arranges them in a circle, a ritual of focus. "They sound like the city," she told her mother once. "If I listen carefully, I can hear the sea talking to the sky."

Above them, the night is clear. Gaza's sky, stripped of electricity, glows with the kind of stars cities elsewhere have forgotten. Astronomers call this phenomenon "dark-sky visibility." Here, it feels more like a gift born of deprivation — a brightness unbought.

For a moment, Layla forgets the statistics, the shortages, the ache of unfinished work. The sea is silver under the moon, the air smells of jasmine and salt, and the sky seems endless — unbroken by drones or borders. "Maybe," she whispers, "this is what freedom looks like."

Omar turns toward her, his expression unreadable. "Freedom," he says slowly, "is when we can sit here and not have to whisper it."

They fall silent, watching as a meteor streak across the horizon — a line of fire too brief for a wish. Mariam gasps, eyes wide. "Did you see that?" she cries. "It's a sign!"

Omar smiles, touching her hair. "It's a promise," he says. "Even the sky remembers us."

The next morning, the city wakes again to the familiar rhythm: the clatter of carts, the hiss of tea, the crackle of radios tuned to the latest news. But for Layla and her family, the memory of that night lingers — a reminder that beyond all the rubble and ration lines, Gaza still owns two infinities: the sea that cannot be silenced, and the sky that refuses to forget.

In both, they find a map not of escape, but of belonging.

For in Gaza, the sea and the sky are not opposites — they are reflections of the same truth: that life, however confined, always finds a way to rise.

Rebuilding in Gaza means rebuilding memory.

Each wall, each window, is more than a structure — it is a monument to what was lost, and a quiet declaration of what must not be forgotten.

Across the Strip, reconstruction rises in fragments. Concrete mixes with recollection; hammers strike like metronomes of endurance. Families patch bullet holes with tin, paint over cracks with borrowed brushes, and hang bright curtains over shattered glass. The act itself — repetitive, imperfect — becomes a kind of prayer.

In Beit Lahia, houses bloom again in impossible colour. Turquoise, lemon yellow, coral pink — shades that defy the greyness of war. "We paint because we can't plant trees everywhere," one woman explains, her hands still dusted with blue pigment. "Colour keeps us alive."

Children draw suns and flowers on rough cement walls. Their murals bloom along alleyways — gardens that need no rain. A boy sketches a kite rising over the ruins; a girl paints a door that leads to the sea. Their art becomes testimony, brushstrokes of belonging.

Women sweep dust from doorsteps that open onto debris, fold blankets with the precision of ritual, and hang embroidered cloths above windows where glass will take months to return. Even the smallest gestures — lighting incense, arranging cups for tea — reassert normalcy in a place where normal has been exiled.

In Khan Younis, an old man named Yusuf spends every morning planting olive saplings beside the rubble of his son's house. His hands tremble, but he presses each root firmly into the earth. "These will see peace," he tells his grandchildren, "Even if I do not." He ties ribbons of fabric to the branches — scraps from his late wife's dresses — so that the wind will remember her scent.

Layla's father rebuilt one corner of their house by hand. At its foundation, he placed a single stone from their family's old home in Shejaiya, long since levelled. He kept it wrapped in cloth for years — the last remnant of a doorway that once opened to jasmine and laughter. "He remembers it," Layla says softly, "the sound of her voice, the smell of bread. He built the new wall so the memory wouldn't fade."

When Omar helped finish the wall, he noticed words faintly scratched into the stone:

"Here began our morning." He traced them with his fingertips, feeling the grain of history beneath the dust. In Gaza, memory is not nostalgia — it is identity, a claim to existence in a place the world often measures only by its destruction. Every repaired roof says we were here. Every coat of paint whispers we still are.

Old photographs survive in biscuit tins and plastic bags, guarded like relics. People keep keys to homes that no longer exist, deeds to lands now fenced and renamed. On shelves beside bread and medicine sit wedding photos, report cards, a seashell from Jaffa — fragments of continuity that outlast the rubble.

In a refugee camp near Deir al-Balah, a grandmother keeps a faded postcard of Jerusalem taped to her mirror. "I've never been," she says, "but my mother was born there. When I brush my hair, I tell her reflection we haven't forgotten."

Rebuilding in Gaza is never just construction. It's inheritance — a ritual of defiance against erasure. The sound of hammers becomes the pulse of memory; the scent of wet cement mingles with thyme and diesel, marking the intersection of survival and history. And when dusk falls, and the muezzin's call floats over the half-built rooftops, the light catches on painted walls — blue, yellow, and pink — shimmering like small flags of resilience. Here, even ruins breathe. Even dust remembers names. And every brick laid by trembling hands becomes part of a larger story — a story that says, again, we build, therefore we remain.

Part 8 — Hope as Architecture

In 2020, the world came to a sudden halt. Cities that once pulsed with motion fell silent beneath the weight of a virus that respected no borders. Airplanes were grounded, streets emptied, and people everywhere learned the language of distance — masks, isolation, uncertainty. From New York to New Delhi, fear became the common tongue. Windows filled with candles and applause for nurses; balconies became stages for songs of endurance. For a moment, humanity shared a single truth — that fragility was universal, that breath itself was precious. Yet while much of the world locked itself indoors, Gaza could not. For Gaza, lockdown was not new; it was a way of life long before the word became global vocabulary.

Gaza remained under blockade. Its borders — both visible and invisible — hemmed in every dream. The airspace, the coastline, the crossings: all under control, all under watch. Poverty surpassed 53 percent, unemployment hovered above 46 percent, and two-thirds of Gaza's youth had never set foot beyond the Strip. Yet amid this confinement, renewal began to bloom in small, deliberate acts — like weeds forcing their way through concrete.

In Khan Younis, volunteers rebuilt classrooms using salvaged doors and repurposed glass. In Deir al-Balah, a clinic reopened with solar panels donated by diaspora engineers. Across Rafah, new roofs gleamed under the sun, patchwork silver reflecting both light and defiance. Hope was not loud here; it whispered through hammer blows, through the soft sweep of brooms over new tiles, through the steady rhythm of hands refusing to rest.

For Omar and Layla, hope took root on their own rooftop. They planted jasmine, mint, and basil in old paint cans, arranging them beside Mariam's small telescope. The plants softened the skyline — a fragile green against Gaza's endless grey. At dusk, the scent of jasmine mingled with the sea breeze, rising above the hum of generators and the distant clatter of rebuilding.

Each evening, when the power cuts rolled across the city, Mariam would sit beside her mother, watching the sky flicker between light and darkness. One night, as the stars appeared — faint, scattered, shy — she asked, "Mama, do the stars see us?"

"Yes," Layla whispered. "And they remember." The words lingered in the still air like a prayer.

For in Gaza, rebuilding is not merely physical — it is spiritual. It is a declaration that faith and endurance can outlast siege. Every wall rebuilt is a psalm, every repaired roof an act of devotion. Hope becomes architecture: the belief that a house can hold love again, that a seed will grow despite the dust, that tomorrow will arrive — late, but certain.

Omar's cooperative joined a UNDP project rebuilding housing in Beit Hanoun. Their work was slow, often interrupted by shortages or blackouts, but he treated each brick as testimony.

"A wall," he said, "is a sentence in the language of survival."

When cement ran out, they used clay mixed with straw; when steel was blocked, they recycled metal from old beams. Out of scarcity, they built endurance.

One afternoon, a foreign journalist visited the site, taking photos of the unfinished houses. She asked Omar what kept him going. He wiped sweat from his brow and answered simply,

"Because I want my daughter to see the sky through a window, not through rubble."

In another part of the city, Layla's students began painting murals on rebuilt walls — poems by Mahmoud Darwish, verses from the Qur'an, drawings of kites and open doors. Some wrote "We are still here" in both Arabic and English. The murals turned streets into stories, colour into resistance.

Hope in Gaza is practical, almost scientific. It survives by adapting — like plants growing sideways toward any shaft of light. It is found in the women teaching coding from laptops powered by car batteries, in the fishermen who still sail past curfews, in the children who plant seeds in buckets and call them forests.

Layla once wrote in her notebook: "We rebuild not because the struggle is over, but because it continues. And in our rebuilding, we defy it."

That defiance is the architecture of Gaza — built from patience, persistence, and prayer. Every hammer strike echoes both past and promise. Every completed home is more than shelter; it declares resilience and freedom.

They rebuild because to live — even under siege — is to resist. And in every wall that rises, every window that opens to the wind, there is a quiet vow whispered in stone:

We will not be erased.

1.5 CHAPTER 4 – UNDER THE RUBBLE: STORIES OF LOSS AND RESILIENCE

"Even the rubble blooms. Beneath every broken wall, a root waits for rain."
— *From graffiti on Al-Wehda Street, Gaza City, 2021*

Part 1 – The Day the Ground Moved

The sky over Gaza was pale and silent that morning — the kind of silence that carries weight, like a breath being held by the entire city. Even the wind seemed to hesitate. Seagulls circled over the shore, their cries sharper than usual, echoing off cracked rooftops.

Layla had just set a pot of mint tea on the stove when the sound began — a faint, metallic hum that vibrated through the window glass. She froze mid-motion, her hands hovering above the cup. Every Gazan knows that sound; it doesn't need translation. It's the sound that enters your bones long before your mind catches up — the sound that says run.

Omar, standing by the window, instinctively began counting.

Three.

Two.

One.

The world convulsed.

The explosion tore through the neighbourhood like a fist made of fire. The floor jumped under their feet, the windows burst inward, and the air filled with the scream of shattering glass. A shockwave slammed through the walls, hurling the pot of boiling tea into the air. Steam and dust merged into one choking cloud.

Layla didn't think — she moved. Her arms wrapped around Mariam before the child could even cry. She pressed her daughter's face into her chest as another blast thundered somewhere close, the walls groaning, dust raining from the ceiling like ash.

After the rumbling ended, a thick, stifling silence filled the air, interrupted just by the soft hiss of flames. Layla could taste concrete dust on her tongue. The room smelled of smoke, metal, and salt — the smell of fear itself.

Omar pushed open the door and stepped into the stairwell, barefoot. The corridor was filled with smoke and the acrid sting of burning plastic. Down the street, screams carried through the haze. When he reached the balcony, the building across from theirs — Samira's home — was gone. Where her kitchen once stood, there was only a crater filled with grey dust and twisted rebar.

He shouted her name into the smoke. "Samira! Samira!"

Neighbours were already there, running toward the wreckage. Some carried shovels, others just used their hands. The ground was hot. Someone found a torn piece of a curtain; someone else held up a child's shoe covered in ash.

And then — a sound. A faint cry, buried deep beneath the rubble.

"Here! Here!" Omar yelled, his voice breaking.

Men dropped to their knees, clawing through the wreckage with bleeding fingers. Every few seconds, the cry came again — weak, but alive. When they finally reached him, they found Samira's son half-buried under concrete slabs. His small face was grey with dust, his eyelashes coated like frost. His chest rose and fell — barely.

Omar lifted him out, holding him close. "Mama?" the boy whispered. No one answered.

There were no ambulances. The main road was blocked by fallen debris. Volunteers turned carts, bicycles, and even market trolleys into makeshift stretchers. They carried the injured toward a nearby school, which had become an improvised clinic. Inside, desks were turned into operating tables, and doctors worked under the dim glow of phone flashlights until the batteries died.

Layla spent the day helping women bandage wounds with torn bedsheets, pouring water over burns, whispering verses of comfort to mothers who had no children left to comfort. Every scream echoed off the walls, repeating itself endlessly.

When the power flickered back on for one hour that night, Omar called Layla from the schoolyard. His voice trembled with exhaustion. "I found Samira's son," he said softly. "He's alive."

Layla pressed the phone to her ear, her breath caught halfway. "And Samira?" she asked. The silence that followed was long and heavy — the kind of silence that carries a thousand funerals. He didn't answer. He didn't need to.

Layla closed her eyes. In Gaza, silence is the language of grief — and that night, the whole city spoke it. Outside, the sea murmured beyond the smoke, indifferent and eternal. It was the only thing that kept breathing.

Part 2 – Shelter in the School

Two days after the bombing, the family joined hundreds of others in a UNRWA-run school that had been transformed into a temporary shelter. The classrooms, once full of equations and laughter, had become dormitories for the displaced. Chalk dust still clung to the air. On the blackboard in one room, the words *"Midterm Exam: Fractions and Decimals"* were half-erased — a frozen message from a life abruptly interrupted.

The schoolyard, where children once lined up for morning assembly, now held lines of people waiting for aid. UN vehicles, painted white and blue, stood parked outside the gate, their logos already covered in dust.

Inside, each classroom hosted four or five families — sometimes thirty people sharing a space meant for twenty students. The floor was covered in UNHCR tarpaulins and thin foam mattresses. Blankets were hung from wires to carve out corners of privacy that did not really exist. The smell was overwhelming — sweat, fear, disinfectant, and dust — a scent that clung to the skin.

Children tried to make sense of it all. They played with chalk pieces and bottle caps, building small cities that crumbled every time someone walked by. One boy used an old math book to fold paper planes. When it flew across the room and hit Omar's shoulder, he smiled faintly — the first smile in days.

Teachers who once explained grammar and geometry were now relief coordinators, aid distributors, and grief counsellors. A former literature teacher, Samira, drafted short poems on scraps of cardboard and taped them to the classroom walls. One read:

"If we must live inside a school,
Let us remember that learning is survival."

Every evening, volunteers with clipboards walked through the halls, counting families, updating headcounts. Their voices were tired but steady: *"How many here? Any new arrivals? Any medical cases?"*

Layla joined a small team of women who cooked in the courtyard. They built makeshift stoves from tin cans and broken bricks, feeding them with scraps of wood scavenged from the street. The air filled with smoke and the faint smell of lentils. "If we feed the children," Layla said, "they'll believe tomorrow still exists."

Fuel was scarce, so aid trucks brought only a few gas cylinders. Families rationed every flame, every drop of water. One day, a volunteer brought a single box of canned beans and powdered milk for the entire floor. "This is all we have," he said apologetically. Layla divided it carefully — half for dinner, half for morning.

At night, Omar sat by the window with a battery-powered radio, one of the few that still worked. He turned the dial slowly, searching for clear stations amid the static that sounded like whispering ghosts. Al Jazeera, BBC Arabic, Radio Gaza — all carried the same grim rhythm:
"Number of displaced — one million.
Hospitals — out of fuel.

Water pumps — inoperable.
Casualties — rising."

Omar took out his notebook and wrote each figure down, not as statistics but as memory. Next to each number, he scribbled small notes: *"The old man with the blue scarf." "The girl with one shoe." "Layla's student — still missing."*

The nights were long and heavy. The freezing air crept through the broken windows. Cries of children echoed down the corridors — nightmares, hunger, fear. The electricity never came, but in one corner of the hall, a teenager rigged a phone to a solar charger and played soft music. For a moment, it sounded like peace.

Mariam slept close to her mother, clutching her toy — a small cloth doll sewn from a sock and filled with cotton. "Mama," she whispered one night, "why can't we go home?"

Layla brushed her hair, her voice trembling but calm. "Because the house is tired, habit. It needs to rest before we can."

The next morning, Omar helped unload new supplies from a Red Crescent truck — bottled water, hygiene kits, plastic jugs. One of the UN workers told him quietly that some families had been living in schools like this since the 2014 war — never able to rebuild because cement imports were blocked or diverted.

In the courtyard, Layla watched as children stretched their hands out from the doorway, catching raindrops on their palms. She thought, *this is how Gaza survives — by finding small ways to feel alive.*

That night, she added her own note beside Samira's poem on the wall:

"If we must live in ruins,
Let us be the seeds that bloom there."

And as she wrote, the generator coughed once and died —
plunging the school into darkness again. Yet even then,
somewhere in the corridor, a baby began to laugh.

Part 3 – Hospitals Without Sleep

Omar began volunteering at Al-Shifa Hospital, where the
corridors overflowed with the wounded. From the moment he
stepped through the doors, the air itself seemed to shudder —
thick with the smell of blood, disinfectant, and sweat. The echo
of footsteps never stopped; gurneys rattled, monitors beeped,
and voices shouted over the drone of generators.

There were no quiet corners left. Patients lay two deep in the
hallways, some on stretchers, others on the bare floor with IV
bags tied to window bars or taped to the walls. The tiles were
slippery with melted ice from blood bags; the air was hot and
tense.

In one corner, a young mother sat cross-legged beside her son's
bed, whispering verses from the Qur'an while fanning his face
with a folded chart. Nearby, a nurse wiped sweat from her
forehead with the edge of her sleeve before hurrying toward
another room that had no door — just a curtain stained with
soot.

Supplies vanished faster than they arrived. When anaesthetics
ran out, surgeons operated with only morphine and prayer. The
smell of cauterized flesh mixed with the faint sweetness of
antiseptic. Nurses cooled blood bags with melting ice scavenged
from cafeteria freezers. The hum of the generators — deep,
mechanical, uneven — filled every silence like the heartbeat of
something ancient and exhausted.

Omar helped where he could: carrying stretchers, fetching water, mopping blood from the floor. He had never been inside a hospital like this — not one that felt so alive and dying at the same time. The walls absorbed every cry.

A young surgeon named Hassan, barely thirty, stood beside him one night, his gloves red up to the wrists. His eyes were sunken, the whites webbed with veins. His hands trembled slightly as he reached for another instrument. "We work sixteen hours, sleep two," he told Omar, his voice flat from fatigue. "If we stop, people die. If we continue, we might die ourselves. There is no right choice anymore — only duty."

When the lights flickered, no one panicked. Everyone simply kept working, counting the seconds until the generator caught again.

Outside, Layla came each morning to the hospital gate. She carried baskets of bread, dates, and bottles of water wrapped in damp cloth. Security rarely let her through, but she waited in the sun until someone — a nurse, a cleaner, a driver — took the food inside. Her eyes followed the baskets as they disappeared through the metal gates.

An elderly nurse once stopped to thank her. "You feed the healers," she said softly, placing a trembling hand over her heart. "You heal the city."

Every night, Omar returned home long after midnight, his clothes stiff with dust and antiseptic. He would sit in silence, too tired to speak. Then, slowly, he began to write.

In a small notebook already stained and torn, he recorded what he saw — not in full sentences, but fragments:

A boy who lived but lost his leg.

A girl who whispered her father's name until dawn.

A surgeon who fell asleep standing, scalpel in hand.

Prayer at 3 a.m., between two explosions.

He no longer cried. He just wrote, as if the act itself were a form of survival — a way to hold the city together when everything else was falling apart.

Some nights, when the generator stuttered and the world went dark, Omar imagined the hospital as a single, enormous heart — wounded, but still beating. And every person inside, from doctors to cleaners, was another pulse keeping Gaza alive.

Part 4 – The Weight of Dreams

When the ceasefire finally arrived, it was not peace — it was a pause. A breath held between two storms. The explosions stopped, but the echoes remained, drifting through shattered streets like ghosts.

The city looked like a broken map — streets unrecognizable, names erased. According to United Nations estimates, more than 45 percent of Gaza's homes were damaged or destroyed. Whole neighbourhoods — Shuja'iyya, Beit Hanoun, Rafah — were reduced to grey fields of debris. The smell of bread, once carried from morning bakeries, had been replaced by dust and smoke. Even the sea smelled different — burnt, metallic, as if it too had been wounded.

People emerged slowly, blinking against the sunlight, stepping over rubble as if learning to walk again. Children pointed to the sky, surprised to see it still blue.

At night, inside the school-turned-shelter, the air was thick with breath and kerosene smoke. Families huddled on thin mattresses; their belongings packed in plastic bags. The walls were covered with graffiti and chalk drawings — hearts, birds, and words of faith: sabr (patience), amal (hope).

Conversations drifted softly through the dark. They did not talk about politics or war — only the things they had lost.

A favourite coffee mug, still buried under the rubble.

A wedding photo.

A door that creaked every morning like a greeting.

A fig tree that once shaded their courtyard.

Layla dreamt often of their old balcony — the one with the jasmine Omar had tended so carefully. In her sleep, she saw it still standing, fragrant and alive. When she woke, her fists were clenched, her palms damp with tears, as if she had been holding the flowerpot all along.

Omar spent his days helping clear debris from the streets, his hands blistered, his face perpetually grey with dust. Each time he came back to the shelter, Mariam would run to him, pressing her face into his chest. He would whisper, "The city is tired, habibti. But it's still standing."

A few weeks later, psychologists from Médecins Sans Frontières (MSF) arrived. They came not with medicine, but with boxes of crayons, paper, and gentle voices. "Draw what you remember," one counsellor told the children. "Or draw what you wish."

The room filled with the sound of crayons scratching across paper — red for roofs, blue for sky, brown for earth. Some drew houses with walls missing; others drew birds, suns, or hands reaching toward each other.

Mariam sat cross-legged on the floor, her tongue between her teeth in concentration. When she was done, she held up her drawing — a small house with three square windows and a giant yellow sun. On the roof, in uneven handwriting, she wrote: "We live."

The room went silent. The adults stared at the paper, at the trembling letters made by a child's hand. Then, quietly, someone began to clap. Another joined, then another — a hesitant rhythm that grew into applause. For a moment, the shelter felt bright again.

That night, as the candles burned low, Layla whispered to Omar, "Maybe hope is the only thing that doesn't need rebuilding." He nodded, staring at the flicker of light dancing on the cracked wall. "Because it's already inside us," he said. And somewhere in the distance, the sea murmured again — steady, endless, as if to agree.

Part 5 – Rebuilding the Body and the Soul

When the bombs stopped falling, the silence that followed felt heavier than the explosions. It was not relief — it was reckoning. The air still smelled of smoke and salt; every gust of wind carried a memory. Streets once mapped by laughter were now unrecognizable — crooked, collapsed, coated in the pale dust of everything that had been home.

Omar joined a team from UN-Habitat, walking through the city with clipboards and cameras. They moved like ghosts among ghosts, mapping damage block by block — which clinics still stood, which wells still flowed, which walls still whispered life. Every photograph they took felt like an act of witness, a confession written in light and ruin: This happened. We were here.

Sometimes, as he clicked the shutter, Omar caught his own reflection in shattered glass — a man both observer and survivor. He wrote the coordinates of each site carefully in his notebook, as if naming them could protect them from being forgotten again.

Back at the school-shelter, counsellors from the World Health Organization (WHO) and local NGOs began gathering families into circles beneath the faint hum of battery-powered fans. They sat cross-legged on classroom floors, surrounded by chalk drawings of suns and trees.

"What is the first thing you will rebuild?" one counsellor asked gently.

A mother raised her hand. "My kitchen," she said. "If I can cook again, my children will think the war is over." Another woman whispered, "My roof — so the sky won't watch us anymore." The counsellor nodded, writing the words down like prayers. Around them, children slept against the walls, their small faces relaxed for the first time in weeks.

Layla joined a women's workshop organized by a local NGO and the Palestinian Red Crescent, where they taught both first aid and emotional resilience. The sessions took place under a canopy of plastic sheets that flapped in the wind. Women sat with notebooks in their laps, learning how to treat burns, disinfect wounds with saltwater, and calm children during shelling.

They also practiced breathing exercises — inhale peace, exhale fear. It sounded simple, but for Gaza's women, even breathing without fear was an act of courage.

"Every woman here is a nurse now," Layla joked one afternoon, her smile thin but defiant. The others laughed — the brittle, exhausted laughter of people who have forgotten what silence feels like.

That night, when the shelter finally grew quiet, Layla lay under her blanket, the air thick with dust and candle smoke. The laughter from earlier replayed in her head until it broke apart. She pressed her hands to her face and wept silently — not just for what was gone, but for the weight of holding everyone else together.

Omar had begun collecting testimonies from survivors — fishermen, teachers, mothers, children — for a book he promised himself he would one day finish. "So, the world will not forget," he told Layla. Each story came to him like a fragment of light in the dark.

The first line he wrote was simple: "We are not numbers; we are the echo of what was loved." And, as he read it aloud to Layla by candlelight, the wind outside shifted softly, carrying the faint smell of jasmine through the broken window. For a moment, the city seemed to listen — as if Gaza itself were exhaling, rebuilding not just its walls, but its soul.

Part 6 – The Return Home

Three weeks after the ceasefire, the long procession began — families carrying what was left of their lives through streets that no longer resembled their city. Some pushed carts filled with clothes, others balanced mattresses and water jugs on their heads. They were not returning *home*; they were returning to ruins.

Omar carried Mariam on his shoulders so she would not have to see the ground — the glass, the twisted rebar, the ashes where houses had been. Layla walked beside him, clutching a plastic bag filled with keys that opened nothing now, their jagged edges cold against her palm.

They passed the wreckage of familiar places: the corner bakery flattened to a slab, the school where Layla once taught now burned and roofless. A playground was half-buried under rubble, the rusted remains of a swing set dangling in the wind. Someone had written on a surviving wall in black spray paint: "We will rebuild. We have no other choice."

When they reached their street in Shuja'iyya, Omar stopped. For a moment, he couldn't move. The building still stood — somehow — but it was wounded. The northern wall had collapsed, leaving their living room open to the sky. Curtains fluttered from the edge like flags of surrender. The refrigerator lay on its side in the rubble, its door hanging open as if exhaling.

Layla stepped forward slowly, her sandals crunching over broken glass. She recognized the cracked ceramic tiles of their old kitchen. She knelt, brushing away the dust until she found a single blue tile, still smooth beneath her fingertips. She pressed it to her lips and whispered, "It still smells like home."

Above them, a pigeon cooed from the corner of what used to be their ceiling. Mariam pointed and said, "Look, Mama, the birds came back before we did."

Omar exhaled, half laughter, half grief. "Then it's safe enough for us too."

Around them, neighbours emerged from alleys, blinking at the light. Some carried brooms, hammers, and nails; others came with tarps from UNDP and wooden beams from the Red Crescent. Together they began the slow ritual of cleaning and reclaiming.

Aid trucks rolled through the streets, distributing plastic sheeting, rope, and hygiene kits. A UN field officer shouted through a megaphone: "Temporary materials only! Cement permits are still under review!" Everyone nodded, already knowing what that meant — *months* of waiting for paperwork that might never come.

Still, they built.

Men cleared debris with shovels and bare hands. Women swept soot from doorways that no longer had doors. Someone salvaged a half-broken mirror and propped it against a wall; in its cracked reflection, life flickered again.

Children played with the only materials left to them — empty bottles turned into toy cranes, lifting imaginary walls and lowering invisible beams. The sound of their laughter mixed with the rhythmic hammering of reconstruction — a music of defiance.

Omar scavenged from the rubble, found pieces of wood, and bent metal rods. He built a simple wooden frame, nailing it into the wall that once held their living room window. "One day," he told Mariam, "This will be a window again."

Part 7 – Faith and Small Joys

By the first week of June 2021, barely three weeks after the ceasefire, the city began to pulse again — slow, tentative, fragile. Markets reopened in the alleys of Al-Zawiya and Deir al-Balah. Vendors swept away dust from the 11-day bombardment that had killed over 260 people, including sixty-seven children, and injured more than 1,900. They propped up stalls with salvaged wood. The shelves were half-empty, but colour returned: bruised tomatoes, mint, sacks of flour stamped with WFP 2021.

At the harbour, fishermen patched their boats with tin sheets. The Israeli navy had just reinstated the old restriction — six nautical miles from shore. Past that invisible border lay warning shots or arrest. Still, before dawn, the boats went out. The sea smelled of diesel and courage. "We fish with fear and faith together," one man told an AFP reporter.

Electricity flickered for four to six hours a day; the main power plant had run out of fuel during the fighting. Yet on Fridays, when the muezzin's voice carried over the ruins, families climbed to rooftops for tea. Someone always brought a radio tuned to Voice of Palestine. Someone always joked, "When the power cuts, we speak louder so God can hear us."

Layla organized a wedding for two neighbours who had postponed their ceremony during the bombing. It was 18 June 2021, the night before Eid al-Adha preparations began. Fairy lights were strung across broken rebar, and a phone speaker played love songs by Mohammed Assaf. Women clapped, children danced between piles of bricks.

"This," Omar whispered to the groom, "is Gaza's secret weapon. We celebrate before the world says we can."

That night, for the first time, the sound of laughter carried farther than the hum of drones. And for a few fragile hours, the sky above Gaza City belonged to music instead of war.

Part 8 – The Promise of Tomorrow

Months later, the rhythm of life began to return — slow, uneven, but steady. Dust still hung over Gaza like a faint memory, yet from beneath it came the unmistakable sound of rebuilding: hammers striking, drills humming, children laughing on their way to class.

Omar's NGO finally received funding from the European Union's reconstruction programme to rebuild several schools across Gaza City and Khan Younis. The funds arrived late, tangled in bureaucracy, but when the first shipments of concrete and solar panels crossed the border, people cheered. Trucks carrying books and desks rolled through streets that had once echoed with sirens.

Layla returned to teaching — this time in a new classroom with walls of bright white plaster and a roof lined with donated solar panels. The hum of the inverter replaced the old rattle of the generator. On the walls, children's drawings fluttered in the breeze from a single standing fan.

The computers were second-hand — old laptops donated from abroad, patched together with tape and wire, keys missing, chargers held by rubber bands. Yet to the children, they were windows to the world.

"What are you making?" Layla asked a boy hunched over one of the laptops, his fingers flying over the keyboard. He didn't look up. "A game," he said, grinning. "You rebuild a city from rubble. If you finish the game, the city lives again." Layla smiled, her throat tightening. For a moment, she couldn't speak. The sound of typing, the hum of solar energy, the laughter of children — it all felt like a heartbeat returning after too long underwater.

Outside, the school courtyard shimmered in the afternoon sun. Small olive trees planted months earlier had begun to sprout new leaves. Teachers poured water over them from plastic bottles, treating each sapling like a promise.

At home, the jasmine plant Layla had rescued from the ruins bloomed again. Its scent filled their single room, sweet and sharp, wrapping around them like memory itself. The walls were uneven, patched with cement of different shades, but the light that filtered through the curtains was soft — gentle in a way that only Gaza's light could be after war.

That evening, as they sat together beneath the flickering glow of a solar lamp, Mariam asked, "Mama, will there be another war?" Omar, paused, his eyes catching the faint reflection of the lamp in the cracked glass. "Maybe," he said softly. "But remember, every time the walls fall, we build again. That's who we are."

Layla reached for his hand, their fingers still rough from work. "Then we'll fill the silence with stories," she said. And they did — telling, teaching, rebuilding. Layla taught words; Omar built walls; Mariam drew the future in colours brighter than the sky outside.

In the fragile space between destruction and hope, they made a home again — not perfect, but alive. Because in Gaza, survival is not the opposite of loss. It is the art of turning rubble into life. It is the language of those who refuse to disappear. And that night, when the jasmine brushed against the window and the wind carried the faint hum of distant waves, Gaza breathed again — weary, wounded, but still dreaming.

1.6 CHAPTER 5 – WOMEN OF GAZA: COURAGE IN THE EVERYDAY

In Gaza, women do not break — they bend the world back into shape."
— Field note from a UNRWA social worker, 2022.

Part 1 – The Hands That Hold Everything

Morning in Gaza begins with women's footsteps. Before the first adhan — the dawn call to prayer — they move through courtyards and narrow alleys, lighting stoves, sweeping dust, boiling tea. The city wakes in the rhythm of their work: kettles sigh, brooms whisper, buckets thud against courtyard taps that run only during limited hours.

Layla ties her scarf, checks Mariam's schoolbooks, and steps into a street that smells of fresh bread and diesel — the scent of life and survival. The bakery line already curls around the corner like a ribbon of patience. Two doors down, Um Hassan, a widow from Beach Camp, sells cucumbers and tomatoes from a crate balanced on bricks. "We used to have stalls," she says, adjusting her shawl. "Now we have courage."

The water supply arrives only in a two-hour window every two to three days. Families store what they can in plastic barrels, knowing that 96 percent of Gaza's water is unsafe to drink, according to the UN Office for the Coordination of Humanitarian Affairs (OCHA, 2021). Electricity is rationed — four to six hours per day, sometimes less, depending on the fuel reaching Gaza's sole power plant, which has operated below capacity since the 2007 blockade.

Women plan their days like logisticians:
Wash at 6.
Knead at 7.
Charge phones at 8.
Cook before the current dies at 9.

According to the Palestinian Central Bureau of Statistics (PCBS, 2021), 20 percent of Gaza's households are female headed, many because husbands were killed in airstrikes, imprisoned, or forced to seek work abroad. These women manage budgets that barely exist — the average daily income for families under the poverty line is under $4, according to UNRWA — stretching flour rations from the World Food Programme (WFP) and cash-assistance cards from UNRWA to feed families of six, sometimes eight.

On average, 1.2 million people in Gaza — more than half its population — rely on WFP food aid. The parcels contain flour, chickpeas, lentils, and cooking oil stamped with blue logos and expiry dates longer than most ceasefires.

Layla helps her neighbour Fatima apply for a micro-grant from UN Women's Cash-for-Work Initiative, one of the few programs that support female entrepreneurship. Fatima hopes to buy a sewing machine to restart her small tailoring business.

They work on a second-hand laptop whose screen flickers like a candle. The power cuts every forty minutes, so they type fast between outages, saving drafts with the reflex of muscle memory. The router blinks red; the fan groans to a stop. "Electricity teaches us speed," Fatima jokes, fingers flying over the sticky keyboard.

Behind the humour, the bones of exhaustion show — the kind of weariness that comes from planning every moment around the rhythm of absence. Yet they finish before the battery dies. When the current returns for a brief surge, they upload the application, their faces lit by the glow of a screen that feels, for a moment, like sunlight.

Outside, a bread seller calls prices through a tin megaphone: "Three shekels! Fresh from the oven!"

Children chase him down the street, barefoot, laughing.

And above it all — the whir of a distant drone, the hum of generators, the murmur of women comparing the day's schedules — Gaza wakes, exactly as it has for years: Not peacefully, but persistently. Not easily, but beautifully. Because even here, life keeps its appointments.

Part 2 – Healing Without Rest

In the women's ward of Al-Shifa Hospital — Gaza's largest and most burdened medical centre — Nurse Rasha moves like wind through the corridors: fast, invisible, everywhere at once. The hallways echo with the hum of generators and the soft cries of newborns. The walls are pale green, their paint blistered by years of humidity and power cuts.

Rasha hasn't slept a full night in years. She works 16-hour shifts, sometimes more, because the staff is stretched thin. "We used to have three nurses per ward," she says. "Now, if one falls sick, the rest cover until we forget what day it is."

Fuel shortages mean the generators cough and stall without warning. The Gaza Power Plant, crippled by the blockade since 2007, supplies only a fraction of the Strip's needs — around 120 MW, when 450 MW are required, according to the United Nations OCHA (2022). When the lights flicker and machines fall silent, Rasha doesn't panic; she moves. She hand-pumps oxygen for newborns, counts chest compressions in her head, times them with her breath.

"Sometimes I think the mothers breathe for the babies," she tells Layla one afternoon at the hospital gate, accepting a small bag of dates and flatbread. Layla brings them every Thursday, part of a local women's network that cooks for overworked medical staff.

Inside, the whiteboard in the ward reads like a war diary:

Antibiotics — *critically low*

Bandages — *nearly finished.*

Fuel for incubators — *4 hours left.*

Patience — *running out.*

The air smells of antiseptic, sweat, and boiled linen. The hum of ventilators competes with the buzzing of flies.

A woman in labour clutches a rosary, whispering *Ayat al-Kursi* under her breath. Another, younger, hums lullabies between contractions. The midwife sterilizes scissors and clamps in a pot of boiling water over a gas camping stove because the autoclave failed again.

These are not exceptions — this is normal. The World Health Organization (WHO) reports that over 70 percent of Gaza's hospitals rely on emergency generators as their only power source. At least 40 percent of essential medicines are "completely depleted" in storage, including painkillers, antibiotics, and anaesthetics.

And yet, survival rates remain higher than the supplies suggest.

"Because Gazan mothers are stubborn," Rasha laughs, her eyes rimmed red with sleeplessness. "They refuse to lose. Their faith keeps the hearts beating when our machines cannot."

During the July 2021 bombardment, when airstrikes struck near Al-Shifa, Rasha and her team moved premature babies into a basement corridor — forty infants lined in baskets under battery-powered lamps. "We didn't lose one," she says quietly. "We prayed louder than the bombs."

After each shift, she walks home through streets lined with martyr posters, the faces of young doctors, teachers, and volunteers gazing from the walls. She stops at three she knows — a medical student from Khan Younis, a paramedic killed while rescuing others, a neighbour who once sold her bread. She touches the corners of their photos and whispers the same prayer:
"Let us raise them before they bury us."

Then she walks the rest of the way in silence, the sea breeze heavy with the smell of diesel from the hospital's generators.

At home, she collapses fully dressed on her bed, shoes still on, her scrubs marked by sweat and iodine. Her phone rests beside her hand — always charged, always waiting.

Because in Gaza, rest is just another word for readiness.

Part 3 – The Classroom Reborn

Across town, in Beit Hanoun, a school rebuilt with funds from UNRWA and the Qatar Reconstruction Programme opens its doors. The new sign above the gate reads *Al-Amal Preparatory*

Girls' School, though half its letters are already faded from dust and salt air.

Inside, the walls smell of wet plaster and new paint. Desks are mismatched — some salvaged from bombed schools, others donated from abroad. Windows are patched with whatever glass could be found; sunlight spills through them in uneven rainbows that dance across the floor.

The bell is no longer electric. It's a length of steel pipe struck with a wrench, its clang echoing across the courtyard like a heartbeat that refuses to stop.

Layla teaches computer basics in a classroom that feels part lab, part miracle. There are five old laptops — donated through an EU-funded "Education in Emergencies" programme — and twenty-four girls crowded around them in pairs. Their hijabs are neatly pinned, their sneakers scuffed from long walks through debris.

They share chargers like contraband, whispering to each other when the current flickers. The air buzzes with the hum of diesel generators, the tapping of keyboards, and the occasional giggle when a line of code finally works.

Layla writes on the cracked whiteboard: IF (hope == true) THEN keep going; ELSE try again.

"Every code has logic," she tells them. "So does life. If one path is blocked, find another."

When the power fails — which it does, twice each morning — she switches to storytelling. She tells them about Ada Lovelace and Fatima al-Fihri, about Palestinian women who wrote poetry by candlelight. The girls listen, fanning themselves with notebooks as the fans go still.

Outside, the graffiti reads: "Education is Freedom." For these girls, it's not a slogan — it's oxygen.

According to UNESCO (2023), Gaza's female literacy rate is 96.5 percent, one of the highest in the Arab world. Yet the World Bank reports that female unemployment exceeds 60 percent — higher than anywhere else on Earth. Many graduates never find work, but they study anyway, as if learning itself were defiance.

In Gaza, education is rebellion wrapped in routine.

At recess, girls play hopscotch drawn in chalk beside sandbags. A teacher leads them in a song: *"Bil-ilm nabni al-ghad"* — *"With knowledge, we build tomorrow."*

Layla looks out the window at the graffiti again, the sunlight on the broken glass turning the letters into a mosaic. She knows the statistics; she teaches hope anyway.

"Knowledge first," she tells the class. "Jobs will follow when walls fall."

A hand goes up in the back. It's Rima, a 13-year-old whose father was injured during the May 2021 airstrikes. Her voice is small but steady: "And if the walls don't fall, Miss?"

Layla smiles, picking up a piece of chalk.

"Then," she says, "we write programs that walk through them."

Part 4 – Markets and Money

On Fridays, the women's cooperative in Deir al-Balah, central Gaza, hums like a living machine. The sewing machines rattle in uneven rhythm — a chorus powered by a single diesel generator that coughs every few minutes. Scissors click, threads stretch across tables like veins of colour: crimson, turquoise, olive green.

The cooperative began in 2021 with a $2,000 micro-loan from the Palestinian Women's Affairs Centre (PWAC), backed by a UNDP small business grant. At first, there were only four women, one borrowed machine, and a corner of a half-ruined building. Now, five years later, fifteen families depend on its income.

Each woman has her story stitched into the fabric.

Um Rania, who lost her husband in the 2014 war, embroiders traditional *tatreez* — red and black cross-stitch patterns that trace back generations.

Fatima, once a literature teacher, now oversees packaging, quoting poetry under her breath as she ties string around folded garments.

And Layla, balancing her phone on a roll of fabric, manages online orders when the signal allows.

The cooperative's motto — *"We sew, therefore we survive"* — is painted on the wall in Arabic.

Every month, they send a shipment of dresses and embroidered shawls through Kerem Shalom Crossing, Gaza's only functioning commercial gate. Each parcel is delayed, inspected, sometimes held for days. Still, the clothes eventually reach buyers in Italy, Spain, and the UK, sold through a digital platform run by a solidarity group called Made in Palestine, part of a real network that markets crafts from Gaza's artisans.

Each item carries a tag: Made in Gaza — Stitched in Hope.

Buyers abroad send photographs wearing them on sunny streets: a woman posing by the Seine, another under the London rain. The Gazan women print those pictures on A4 paper and pin them to the wall — their window to a world they cannot visit. "Look," one of them whispers, "our colours reached Paris."

Layla manages the orders late at night. She photographs each piece against a white sheet hung from rebar, edits the photos on a cracked Samsung Galaxy A10, and uploads them when the internet stabilizes — usually after midnight, when fewer people share the bandwidth.

Omar teases her, smiling: "You export resilience."

She looks up from her screen, her eyes bright with the blue glow of the phone. "No," she says. "I export stories. And stories pay rent."

When fabric runs short — which it often does, because textile imports are tightly restricted — they improvise. The women cut patterns from UNRWA flour sacks and stitch *tatreez* over the printed logos of wheat sheaves and blue UN emblems. Waste becomes fashion; history becomes income.

During one especially harsh winter, they stitched school uniforms for displaced children from Khan Younis, earning a small UNRWA contract. "It wasn't much money," Layla says, "but when the children smiled in new clothes, it felt like profit."

In the corner, a toddler sleeps beneath the cutting table while her mother hems a sleeve, the rhythm of the needle a lullaby. Outside, the call to prayer mingles with the sea wind and the hum of the generator.

At the end of the day, when the power finally cuts, the room glows by candlelight. Threads glimmer like veins of gold. The women sit together, sipping sweet tea from chipped glasses, laughing quietly.

Their laughter is the softest sound of resistance.

Part 5 – Love as Equality

At home, Layla and Omar move around each other like dance partners in a choreography shaped by circumstance — an unspoken rhythm of survival and tenderness.

He fills the water tank on the roof whenever the pipes sputter to life — only three hours of municipal water every four days, according to Gaza's Coastal Municipalities Water Utility. She checks the solar battery bank, charging phones, lamps, and the old radio before the electricity cuts again. On good days, the current lasts six hours; on bad days, two.

They trade tasks seamlessly: Omar washes dishes while Layla mends Mariam's school uniform by candlelight; she tracks food rations while he fixes the loose tiles near the balcony. When the generator sputters out, they laugh — because the only alternative is despair.

They argue sometimes, but softly — about prices, about politics, about who forgot to charge the fan battery before bedtime. Yet even the arguments feel like partnership.

In a culture still tugged by tradition, where many women remain confined to domestic roles, their marriage is a quiet rebellion. Layla teaches online, earns small income through the sewing cooperative, and manages their finances. Omar, who once resisted the idea of his wife working, now tells neighbours with pride, "She keeps our house running when the world stops."

Theirs is not equality declared in speeches but practiced in errands — a kind of shared endurance.

One evening, as Mariam sleeps under the weak whir of a solar fan, Layla and Omar sit beside her on the floor, the lantern casting long shadows on the walls painted sky-blue.

"You build walls," Layla says softly, "and I build dreams. Together maybe we make a house."

Omar smiles, tapping the lantern's rim. "In Gaza, that's the same thing."

The light flickers, briefly dying, then returns — as if agreeing with him.

Later that week, they queue together outside the bakery at dawn, the smell of yeast and smoke filling the air. A UN report had just noted that 70% of Gaza's households experience food insecurity, but in the line, people still joke, trade news, share tea in paper cups. Layla teases Omar for buying extra bread; he shrugs and says, "For the neighbours — and for your midnight tea."

They move on to the pharmacy, taking turns in the queue for antibiotics for Mariam's cough. A shipment from the World Health Organization had arrived through Kerem Shalom Crossing, but supplies are rationed — one bottle per family. They wait two hours, sharing an umbrella against the midday sun.

At home, Omar carries groceries up four flights of stairs because the elevator hasn't worked in years. Layla opens the window to let in the sound of the sea — that distant hum that reminds them why they never left.

In Gaza, love is measured not in roses but in errands done under sun and sirens. It's in the extra scoop of lentils in the soup pot, the shared generator fuel, the whispered prayer before sleep.

Sometimes, when the sky falls quiet for more than a day, Omar buys a single jasmine flower from a street vendor and tucks it into Layla's book.

He never says *I love you* aloud — the words are too fragile for this place — but when the lights go out and she reaches for his hand in the dark, she already knows.

Part 6 – Faith, Art, and Expression

When the lights die, Gaza glows — not with neon, but with candles, phone screens, and faith. Every home becomes a small lantern against the blackout. In those hours between bombardment and calm, women stitch, sing, write, and pray so that the children can sleep without fear.

Layla's writers' group meets every Thursday evening at the Shammout Cultural Centre in Gaza City, one of the few community spaces rebuilt after the 2014 war. They gather in a circle of plastic chairs, sipping mint tea brewed over a camping stove. The electricity rarely cooperates, but they keep meeting, their voices steady even when the lights fade.

On the table lies a stack of photocopied poems from UNRWA's *Voices of Gaza* — a real anthology first circulated in 2022, displaying poems written by Gaza's youth. One of the youngest members, Huda, a 19-year-old literature student from Shejaiya, reads aloud:

"We are daughters of dust and jasmine; we build lullabies from broken glass."

Her words hang in the air, trembling but unbroken. Everyone applauds softly — not to disturb the children asleep in the next room.

For many here, art has become therapy, memory, and quiet defiance. The Edward Said National Conservatory of Music, funded by the A.M. Qattan Foundation and the EU, continues to train young girls to play violin, oud, and qanun. Their performances stream online to audiences they will never see in person; permits to travel for concerts are impossible to obtain. In 2022, a group of twelve girls performed Bach and Fairuz pieces live on Facebook — by lantern light, during a blackout.

One of Layla's students, Rania, learns to play the oud from YouTube. The internet drops every five minutes, but she rewinds the same lesson, fingers fumbling at first, then finding grace. "When I play," she says, "the world gets bigger than the wall."

Painters in Gaza's Dar al-Nadwa Gallery stretch canvases made from old flour sacks and tent cloth. The Tamer Institute for Community Education donates brushes and small grants. Photographers use donated laptops from UNESCO's "Culture Resilience in Gaza" project to process their images — portraits of life continuing amid rubble, weddings in half-built homes, children chasing kites through destroyed alleys.

Embroidery collectives like Women in Hebron and Sulafa Embroidery Centre, both with branches in Gaza, weave red-and-black *tatreez* patterns — ancestral Palestinian stitches — over recycled fabric from UNRWA food sacks. Each piece carries a story, each stitch a name.

And still, new art appears in the streets. One morning, on a wall shattered by shrapnel near al-Rimal, a mural blooms overnight: a door painted where none exists. Beneath it, someone has written in blue spray paint: "Open Anyway."

No one claims it, but everyone knows who made it — a group of anonymous street artists called "Zawiya," inspired by

Banksy's visits to Gaza. Their murals speak for the voiceless, turning debris into declaration.

To leave Gaza — even for a day — is an ordeal. Permits are controlled by the Coordination of Government Activities in the Territories (COGAT), the Israeli authority that regulates movement through the Erez Crossing in the north and the Rafah Crossing with Egypt in the south.

Women applying for medical or educational travel submit documents through the Palestinian Civil Affairs Office, then wait — sometimes for weeks, sometimes for months — for an answer that may never come. Many are denied without explanation; others receive approval too late — *after the surgery date, after the scholarship deadline, after the conference is over.*

According to WHO reports (2022–2023), nearly one in four medical permit requests from Gaza are denied or delayed, and patients needing urgent cancer or cardiac care often miss treatment appointments. In 2022, 63 Gazans died while waiting for medical exit permits — 38 of them women or children.

Rasha, the nurse, once received permission for a maternal-health training in Jerusalem, sponsored by the World Health Organization and UNFPA, but her permit arrived two months too late. She framed the invitation letter, anyway, hanging it above her bed — a diploma in patience. "Even our learning is blockaded," she sighs.

Layla mentor's younger women chasing the few scholarships that escape Gaza's walls. She runs evening sessions in the community centre at al-Rimal, lit by solar lamps. Together they draft essays by candlelight, scan passports in a copy shop powered by panels donated by Norwegian Church Aid, and refresh inboxes like prayer.

One girl, Dina, dreams of studying environmental engineering in Türkiye. After her third rejection from COGAT, she slumps over her keyboard. "Why try?" she whispers. Layla squeezes her shoulder. "Because they'll remember our names. Paper is patient — and so are we."

Cultural norms form another layer of the wall. Some fathers still hesitate to let their daughters travel alone or work night shifts in NGOs. But necessity changes hearts. Since 2020, male unemployment has hovered around 45–50%, while women's home-based work has become an economic lifeline. Faith leaders, too, have adapted. Imams on local radio quote Prophet Muhammad's (peace be upon him) saying: *"Seeking knowledge is a duty upon every Muslim — male and female."* Religion becomes a bridge, not a barrier.

Activists form a youth group called "Girls for Green Gaza," inspired by environmental collectives like Youth Climate Ambassadors (Gaza) and We Are Not Numbers. The girls plant saplings in bomb-scarred lots across Khan Younis and Beit Lahia, watering them with bottles carried from home. Sometimes police question them; sometimes neighbours whisper. Still, they keep planting.

They write their motto on scraps of cardboard and tape it to the gate: "We water the future."

One afternoon, Layla joins them under the harsh June sun. Together, they plant an olive sapling beside a school wall still pocked with bullet holes. A girl kneels to press soil around the roots with bare hands. "This one is for my mother," she says. "She always wanted a tree that would outlive the war."

Layla looks at her and smiles. "Then it already has."

Part 8 – Closing Reflections: The Future in Their Hands

One evening, the community centre hosts an exhibit titled *Fragments of Hope*. Photos line the walls: a woman welding a metal frame; a midwife catching a newborn by lantern light; teenagers coding beneath a solar lamp; a grandmother selling jars of pickled turnips the colour of sunrise.

Layla stands before her own photograph — one hand on a laptop, the other holding Mariam's fingers as they cross a muddy street. A journalist asks, "What keeps you here?"

"Because Gaza needs witnesses," she answers. "If we leave, who will tell the truth?"

That night on the rooftop, rare uninterrupted power hums like a blessing. The air tastes of salt and jasmine. Mariam traces constellations she learned online. "Will you write more stories, Mama?"

"Yes," Layla says. "I will write until the world listens."

Somewhere a generator sputters, then steadies. In that fragile light, the women of Gaza continue their quiet revolution — educating, healing, feeding, loving. Their courage isn't the kind that fills headlines; it's the kind that keeps a city breathing when everything else tries to stop its heart. And in the ledger of survival, it is their handwriting that turns the page.

1.7 CHAPTER 6 – THE CHILDREN OF THE BLOCKADE: GROWING UP BETWEEN WARS

"They learn the alphabet with one hand and hold fear with the other."
— Teacher's Diary, Gaza City 2022

Part 1 – Morning in the Classroom

Morning in Gaza arrives with the metallic whine of generators rising before the call to prayer — a sound so constant it has become part of childhood. The hum weaves through alleys and over rooftops, competing with the shrill bell of Al-Amal Primary School in Beit Lahiya, where the day begins not with certainty, but with endurance.

The school itself is a monument to persistence. Rebuilt after the May 2021 bombardment with support from UNRWA, UNICEF, and the Qatar Charitable Foundation, it stands like a patched-up memory — its walls painted bright yellow to hide the pockmarks of shrapnel, its playground fenced with recycled pipes, its windows trembling with every gust of wind. Cartoon murals stretch across the walls — smiling suns, dolphins, olive branches — each one drawn to cover a crack left by war.

Inside, forty children crowd into a classroom built for twenty-five. The air is thick with heat and diesel, the smell of chalk blending with the tang of fuel from the generator in the courtyard. Each desk holds two or three children; some sit on the floor; pencils gripped like talismans.

Mariam sits near the window; her braid tied with a faded ribbon salvaged from a parcel her uncle once sent from abroad. The pages of her notebook are lined not only with words but with tiny drawings — flowers, hearts, birds — symbols of a freedom she's never seen. In the margin beside her English lesson, she has written Dream three times, circling it in red.

Outside the window, her father Omar works on the new playground fence, welding together pieces of old water pipes for a UNICEF "Back to Learning" project. Sparks fall like fireflies around him, and for a moment, it looks as though the fence itself is being stitched with light. The old swings were melted in the 2021 firestorm that reduced fifty schools to rubble across the Gaza Strip.

Next door, Layla stands at the blackboard in a room without full electricity. The power cuts mid-lesson, the lights flicker, but her voice never wavers. She writes PEACE in broad white letters, sunlight from the cracked glass landing across the board like a fragile blessing.

"Repeat after me," she says.

"Peace," the children chant — their voices uneven, but clear.

"What does it mean?"

A boy near the back raises his hand. "It means no planes."

The room falls silent. For a few seconds, even the generator seems to pause. Layla breathes slowly, steadying herself, and adds another word beneath it: Tomorrow.

According to UNICEF (2022), more than 80 percent of Gaza's children show symptoms of psychological distress — anxiety, sleep disorders, or chronic fear. Teachers have become more than educators; they are psychologists, protectors, and storytellers, trained under Education in Emergencies programs. Their classrooms double as sanctuaries — places where children learn to trust silence again.

A slammed door can empty a room. Thunder can send every child scrambling under their desks, heartbeats synchronising with the memory of drones. And yet, by mid-morning, laughter returns — quiet, hesitant, but unmistakably alive.

During recess, Mariam trades crayons with her best friend, Hala. They sit against a wall still etched with soot, the faint smell of burnt wood lingering in the breeze.

"I want the red," Mariam says.

"Red is too strong," Hala replies softly. "Take blue. Blue is calm."

They begin to draw — a house, a sea, a bird flying. The crayons leave bright streaks on worn pages. For them, colours are not decoration; they are therapy. Every line drawn is an act of defiance, every page a small rebellion against the grey that surrounds them. In Gaza, childhood is not postponed — it persists, fragile but radiant, like a candle that refuses to go out no matter how strong the wind.

Part 2 – Playgrounds of Concrete

There are no soft fields in Gaza. The ground beneath every child's step remembers the weight of something that once fell.

Before each new school term, UNMAS (United Nations Mine Action Service) teams sweep the playgrounds and open lots — men in thick vests and visors combing through sand and rubble with metal detectors. Their beeping instruments pierce the morning air, echoing between broken walls. Between 2009 and 2023, they cleared more than 10,000 unexploded items — mortars, shells, small metallic fragments disguised as toys.

The children watch them sometimes from behind the fences, whispering to each other, "They're finding the sleeping bombs." They have learned to stay away from anything shiny, to treat the world like a puzzle made of danger. Still, when the workers leave, they play.

They make footballs from knotted plastic bags and tape, kick them across uneven courtyards where the goalposts are painted bricks. They draw hopscotch grids with charcoal on cracked cement, the numbers fading each time the rain comes — though rain itself is rare. A crater becomes a goal; a pile of sand becomes a slide. The laughter that follows is as sharp and fleeting as the sparks from Omar's welding torch.

In one empty lot where a building once stood, children have turned ruin into recreation. They leap from stone to stone, calling the gaps between them "the sea." Their games are geography lessons in resilience.

Omar watches Mariam from across the street as she chases a kite made from a torn flour sack stitched together with fishing line. The kite wobbles at first, then catches the wind, rising unevenly but higher with each tug. The white cloth flutters against a sky the colour of pale ash, its corners patched with tape and hope.

"One day she'll fly higher," Omar murmurs — not sure whether he means the kite or his daughter.

Nearby, the muezzin's call echoes through the alleys, merging with the laughter of children. For a moment, the city sounds alive again — fragile, unarmoured, almost normal.

At dusk, the generator hums back to life, filling the apartment with its steady growl. Layla sits by candlelight, writing in her worn notebook. The air smells of kerosene and mint tea. Outside, the kite still hangs in the twilight, snagged in a tangle of wires, its tail trembling with the evening breeze.

She writes: "Children here are born bilingual — fluent in laughter and loss. They play between ruins as if joy were their only weapon. And maybe it is."

Part 3 – Health and Hunger

The paediatric ward of Al-Shifa Hospital hums with exhaustion — the kind of hum that carries through skin and sleep. The air is thick with disinfectant and sweat, a bitter antiseptic scent that clings to every surface. In the corridor, generators tremble under strain, their deep growl rising and falling with the flicker of the fluorescent lights. Power cuts slice the day into fragments.

The hospital runs at 120 percent capacity, its fuel rationed through the WHO Emergency Health Cluster. Each litre is measured like medicine. Monitors blink and stall when the current dips; incubators share power through tangled extension cords. Doctors move through the halls like shadows, stethoscopes clattering against empty oxygen tanks.

Nurse Rasha, her palms cracked from bleach, moves between the cots, her footsteps soft against the tiles. She lifts a toddler whose ribs rise like reeds under his skin. "He just needs milk," she whispers, checking the scale, "and peace."

But milk costs twice what it did before the closure of Kerem Shalom Crossing, Gaza's main commercial artery. Prices soar with every border delay; shelves empty before salaries arrive. A litre of baby formula becomes a treasure. Mothers boil tea leaves to trick their infants' stomachs into quiet.

Layla spends her mornings with UNRWA's women's network, distributing vitamin supplements and fortified flour donated by the World Food Programme (WFP). The community hall smells of sweat, iron, and powdered milk. Dozens of mothers line up silently, their faces veiled with fatigue, each holding a child wrapped in whatever fabric is clean. One woman rocks her baby and says softly, "We wash the air out of them before they sleep — it's all we can give."

Outside, Omar helps the volunteers unload aid trucks at the Kerem Shalom checkpoint. The bags are printed with the familiar blue UN logos, symbols of lifelines rationed by geopolitics. "This flour is older than some of the kids," he jokes, his voice gentle, trying to pull a smile from the workers. Laughter travels across the yard, small and tired, but real.

By dusk, the hospital wards glow faintly under backup lights. The call to prayer echoes faintly through open windows, mingling with the mechanical rhythm of ventilators. Layla sits by the balcony, her journal open, the candlelight trembling across the page. She listens to the hum of the generator, the distant sirens, the sound of Omar's boots outside, and writes: "Hunger isn't only for food — it's for safety, for quiet, for the feeling of tomorrow.

In Gaza, even the full stomach dreams of peace."

Part 4 – Dreams Online

The internet, when it works, is Gaza's only open border.

It's a thin, invisible lifeline — a thread that connects a walled strip of land to the vastness beyond. In a place where every physical crossing is monitored, digital connection becomes its own act of freedom.

By 2024, internet penetration in Gaza reached 78 percent, according to the Palestinian Central Bureau of Statistics, yet the experience remains fragile. Bandwidth fluctuates with power outages; routers hum on battery banks; and during bombardments, entire neighbourhoods go offline for days. Most connections run through ageing 3G networks, still slower than those of the rest of the region, while families save data like food — rationed carefully, shared between phones, borrowed between friends.

Still, for many, the screen is a window to the world.

Mariam studies science on a donated tablet — part of UNICEF's Education in Emergencies program, which distributed more than 60,000 devices to children after schools were damaged or destroyed. The signal flickers, but she persists, joining a virtual classroom linking students from Gaza, Kenya, and Malaysia. Her teacher's voice stutters through static, then disappears. Mariam waits, patient as always, then scribbles note in a frayed notebook to ask later.

"The world is bigger than the wall," Layla reminds her.

Mariam nods, eyes still on the frozen image of her classmates. "One day, I'll see it."

In the evenings, when the power returns for a few hours, she watches YouTube tutorials about coding and astronomy. Her favourite channel is run by a girl in Italy with a golden puppy named Luna. Mariam laughs at the dog's antics, her eyes glowing in the pale screen light. "When we rebuild," she says, "I'll have one too."

Omar kisses her forehead. "Then I'll build it a doghouse with no roof," he says, smiling. "So, it can see the stars."

Technology here is rebellion — not against faith or tradition, but against silence. It keeps Gaza's children connected when roads are closed, when schools are rubble, when the world thinks they've disappeared.

Layla's students form WhatsApp study groups, sharing photos of textbook pages and voice notes recorded in candlelight. "Signal's back," someone writes, and a cascade of messages follows — equations, poems, jokes, hope.

When the Tamer Institute for Community Education launched its Digital Library for Gaza in 2023, usage surged immediately. Thousands logged on to read stories in Arabic and English — tales of astronauts, sea explorers, and ancient poets. Layla noticed her students quoting these lines in essays, mixing mythology with modern dreams. "Technology," she told them, "Is not just about machines. It's about memory — and where we decide to store it."

Online counselling has also become a lifeline. UNICEF and UNRWA jointly operate digital mental health programs, offering chat-based support to youth dealing with trauma. In 2024 alone, more than 40,000 sessions were recorded across Gaza and the West Bank. For many children, those text messages are their first safe space to describe nightmares — of drones, darkness, and loss.

One afternoon, the internet goes out completely. No classes, no messages, no light except the faint sun through dusted windows. Mariam sighs and closes her tablet. "We're offline," she says quietly.

Layla smiles. "Then we dream the old way — with words."

They take turns reading by candlelight, tracing constellations on paper instead of screens. Outside, the city hums its usual rhythm — generators, footsteps, the echo of the sea. Inside, another kind of connection takes place: one built from voices, not cables.

When the signal finally returns at midnight, Mariam's tablet pings with messages. Her classmates have been waiting for her — one from Nairobi, one from Kuala Lumpur, one from Khan Younis. "We missed you," they write. "The world feels smaller when you're here."

Mariam types back, grinning: "I'm still here. Always online, even when the light goes."

In Gaza, education travels through wires when borders will not open. And in those glowing screens — fragile, flickering, alive — the next generation builds bridges no wall can block.

Part 5 – When Night Falls

When night comes, Gaza hums.

The power cuts arrive without announcement, like a tide the city has learned to anticipate. One by one, the lights flicker and die, leaving the streets bathed in the dull orange of battery lanterns and generator sparks. From balconies and rooftops, families ignite candles in chipped glass cups — tiny constellations of survival.

The generators start soon after: low, uneven, metallic throbs echoing through alleys. The city beats to this nervous rhythm, a pulse of persistence beneath a sky that rarely rests. Diesel smoke hangs in the air, mingling with the scent of cardamom tea and salt drifting from the sea.

Inside their apartment, Layla sets the kettle on a small gas stove. The blue flame sputters, fragile but steady. Omar sits by the window, his tools set aside, and Mariam curls up beside her mother, sketching quietly in her notebook. The lantern light dances across their faces — a soft, trembling illumination that makes the room feel sacred.

Omar begins to tell one of his stories, his voice slows and deliberate, as if language itself needs to tread carefully through the dark.

"There was once a fisherman," he says, "who cast his net into the sea at dawn and pulled up gold coins instead of fish. He shared them with everyone in his village, but the next morning, when he tried again, the sea was empty."

"Why?" Mariam asks, eyes wide.

"Because" Omar smiles faintly, "some miracles happen only once. The rest, we must make with our own hands."

Layla laughs softly, then opens a book of old folktales. Her voice joins his — one story blending into another — tales of prophets crossing deserts, birds carrying letters of peace, women outwitting kings. The words weave through the room like a lullaby. On the wall, their shadows move gently, as if the stories themselves have come alive.

Outside, drones hum — distant, insect-like, ever-present. Their sound is so constant it becomes a kind of weather. Sometimes sirens wail, and the whole neighbourhood freezes. Mothers count seconds between blasts, their lips moving in silent prayer. And when the silence returns — the long, aching silence — children slowly pick up their crayons again. They draw suns over rubble, flowers over broken walls, homes with open windows.

"Mama," Mariam whispers, her pencil pausing mid-line, "why do the lights always go off?"

Layla smiles, her voice soft but unwavering. "So, we can see the stars better."

Mariam looks out the window. Above the faint smoke and city dust, a handful of stars pierce the sky — distant, indifferent, eternal.

Omar watches them both. He thinks of the world beyond these walls — cities that never lose power, skies unbroken by drones, people scrolling through headlines before sleep. Somewhere, the lights of London gleam across the Thames. In New York, late commuters ride home beneath neon. In Tokyo, vending machines glow on quiet streets. And here, in Gaza, his daughter sketches by candlelight.

He wonders if anyone, at that very moment, feels the hum of his generator through the cables of conscience. If anyone hears this city breathing through smoke and static.

The contrast stings him — the simultaneity of living. Somewhere, a child is falling asleep to a lullaby on a phone app; here, his child falls asleep to the whir of drones. Somewhere, lovers watch the northern lights; here, they trace light through blackout curtains.

He looks at Layla — the woman who turns fear into poetry — and feels the weight of every silence she has softened with words. She is luminous, not in the way of stars, but in the way of embers — quiet, enduring, alive.

When the power briefly returns, the fan stirs and the refrigerator hums back to life. The lights blink on, too bright for a moment. Mariam blinks against them and whispers, "The stars are gone."

Layla kisses her hair. "They're not gone," she says. "They're just waiting for the next dark."

Omar reaches for her hand, the warmth grounding him against the cold flicker of the world beyond. He knows morning will bring new shortages — of fuel, of food, of patience — but tonight, in this fragile light, they have made something whole again: a story, a moment, a reason to keep going.

Outside, the city hums — a thousand small lights trembling in defiance of the dark. And somewhere, the world turns in its sleep, unaware that while it dreams, Gaza endures.

Part 6 – Trauma and Healing

Every Tuesday, counsellors from UNICEF's Mental Health and Psychosocial Support Programme, in partnership with Save the Children and the Tamer Institute for Community Education, arrive at Gaza's schools with cardboard boxes full of crayons, colouring paper, and something rarer than supplies — permission to feel.

They unpack their boxes slowly, gently, as if handling light. The air smells of chalk, dust, and faint detergent from freshly cleaned floors. The teachers help clear space between desks. The counsellors say the same words each week, rehearsed and hopeful: "Draw what you feel." And the children begin.

Some sketch houses with smoke rising from them, crooked and grey, their windows shaped like eyes. Others draw suns that take up the entire page, blazing in orange and yellow. One boy draws a tree whose roots reach the bottom of the paper, anchoring it as if to stop the world from slipping away.

Mariam always draws the sea. The counsellor kneels beside her, noticing the careful blues she shades again. "Why the sea?" she asks. Mariam doesn't look up. "Because" she whispers, "it's the only thing that never leaves." Her answer settles in the air like a prayer.

Across Gaza, the sea is the same constant. When everything else burns, it remains — not untouched, but undefeated. It holds the voices of the lost, the laughter of those who survived, the reflections of every star that refused to fall.

According to Save the Children's 2023 report "Trapped", four out of five children in Gaza — 80 percent — live with depression, grief, or PTSD-like symptoms. Bed-wetting, nightmares, speech loss, anxiety at loud sounds — all have become part of childhood here. What elsewhere would trigger alarm is simply called "normal."

The counsellors know that trauma in Gaza doesn't end when the bombing stops. It lingers in muscle memory, in unfinished homework, in children flinching at thunder. One girl refuses to colour in red — she says it's too loud. Another insists on using only blue and green, because "they are quiet."

During one session, a boy draws a playground full of swings and writes under it, "When we play, the world forgets to fight." His teacher frames it on the wall.

Layla helps with these sessions whenever she can. She organises storytelling nights at the Community Centre in al-Rimal, supported by the Tamer Institute. The centre has no proper lights — only a solar lamp and a string of LEDs powered by a car battery — but children come anyway, gathering cross-legged on thin mats, faces tilted toward her voice.

She begins with folktales her grandmother once told during curfews: stories of the hoopoe bird who carried messages between kings, of prophets who followed stars through the desert, of the olive tree that remembered every name spoken beneath it.

As she reads, something changes in the room. Shoulders drop. Breathing slows. The rhythm of her voice becomes an anchor in the chaos outside. A boy interrupts. "Are these stories true?" Layla smiles, her voice trembling just enough to be human.

"They're true when you believe them," she says. "Like peace." The children nod, half-understanding, half-dreaming.

When the stories end, the counsellors collect the drawings. Some are smudged with crayon dust; some are folded carefully like letters. They will later be scanned and uploaded to the Gaza Children's Archive, a digital project run by young volunteers who want the world to see what childhood looks like under siege.

Outside, the night deepens. The hum of drones blends with the sound of waves. Inside, the children's laughter lingers — brief, bright, defiant.

Layla locks the centre door and walks home under a sky the colour of ash. She carries the last drawing in her bag — Mariam's Sea, vast and endless. She holds it close, as if the ocean itself could fit on paper.

When she reaches home, Omar is waiting by the window. "Another long night?" he asks.

"Not long," she answers, placing the drawing on the table. "Just wide — like the sea."

He looks at the sketch, at the lines drawn by a child who has seen too much, and says quietly, "Then maybe the sea remembers us, too." And in that moment — between sorrow and survival — healing takes its shape: not as recovery, but as remembrance.

In Gaza, therapy isn't a room or a diagnosis. It's a shared story, a hand steadying another hand, a child's crayon tracing waves that will always return.

Part 7 – Generational Dreams

By adolescence, imagination itself bends around the blockade.

Dreams must learn the geography of limits. Teenagers in Gaza grow up in a place they have never left — where the horizon is always visible but always forbidden. They learn early how to dream within borders, to build futures in fragments.

Omar mentors a group of high-schoolers who meet three afternoons a week at a café powered by solar panels — one of the few left functioning after years of fuel shortages. The panels were donated under a UNDP renewable-energy grant, part of a pilot project to create "green micro-hubs" across Gaza's neighbourhoods. The café hums with the sound of laptops and ambition.

The students design things that should be impossible with what little they have:

A water filter made from sand, charcoal, and discarded plastic bottles.

A solar oven built from mirrors found in a scrapyard.

A mobile app that maps water availability by neighbourhood.

One boy, no older than sixteen, grins as he explains his project. "If we can't import," he says, "we'll invent."

Their Wi-Fi signal flickers as they upload code to a cloud server. The lights dim. No one moves. They've learned to keep working through outages, their persistence as steady as their heartbeat.

Omar watches them, his pride mixed with something heavier — the weight of what they deserve, and what the world withholds. He remembers his own youth under curfew, sketching houses on cement walls because paper was too precious. Now, these teenagers write programs, design drones, and speak of "future markets." He wonders what they could become if the sky itself didn't close around them.

Across town, Layla meets with a circle of older girls in the back room of the community centre. The room smells of tea and photocopier ink. They sit at a wooden table covered in application forms — Amideast, Chevening, Erasmus+, Fulbright — pathways to distant classrooms they have only seen online.

Layla helps them scan IDs on a flickering printer, types of recommendation letters by the light of a rechargeable lamp. Each form asks for a passport number, an airport of departure, a border that must open. Every step feels both thrilling and cruel: hope, written in bureaucratic ink.

One girl, Huda, reads aloud her personal statement: "I want to study environmental engineering so I can bring clean water to Gaza."

Her voice wavers halfway through. "But what if they never let me leave?"

Layla looks at her, steady and firm. "Then you study anyway. Hope is our only visa."

They all laugh softly, but the laughter carries an ache — the kind that comes from dreaming too hard against the odds.

That night, back home, Mariam sits by the window with her notebook. The room is dark except for the glow of her small lamp. The sound of distant waves drifts through the air.

She begins her diary: "When I grow up, I will be a doctor, a writer, and a bird."

She draws two tiny wings beside her name, careful, symmetrical, determined. Her handwriting is round, still childlike, but her tone already carries the calm of someone who has seen too much and still chooses wonder.

Omar watches her from the doorway. "What kind of bird?" he asks.

"The kind that doesn't need a border," she says without looking up.

He feels the words settle inside him like a truth he's been waiting to hear. Later that night, as they lie in bed listening to the hum of distant drones, he whispers to Layla, "Maybe she'll be the first to fly." Layla smiles, tired but luminous. "Then we'll wave from below."

Outside, the sea murmurs against the shore — the same sea that traps them, the same sea that reflects the stars they teach their children to count. Somewhere far away, the world debates politics and ceasefires, but here, under a blackout sky, a new generation is already inventing freedom.

They are the children of siege, the coders of light, the architects of tomorrow's Gaza. And even in a place where walls define everything, they have begun to draw wings that no one can cage.

Part 8 – Closing Reflections: The Meaning of Childhood

Childhood in Gaza is measured not in years, but in ceasefires.

Every child here knows the language of war before learning cursive. They can tell the difference between the buzz of a surveillance drone and the thunder of rain. They grow up counting the seconds between blasts, between blackouts, between aid deliveries that mean the difference between hunger and survival.

Yet somehow — through exhaustion, through grief — they remain children.

At dawn, the streets fill with their laughter. Barefoot boys kick footballs stitched from old socks. Girls braid ribbons into each other's hair, comparing stickers of cartoon characters shared over WhatsApp. They skip rope beside the walls of ruined buildings, their songs bright and off-key. Every smile is defiance, every game, an act of peace.

UNICEF estimates that as of 2025, one million children in Gaza require psychological support, many living with trauma that began before they could form full memories. Over half have known displacement more than once. And yet, teachers report that attendance at reopened schools exceeds 90 percent — because for children here, learning is a rebellion against disappearance. Mariam writes in her diary: "We are not waiting for peace. We are practicing it."

Her words echo a larger truth. Childhood in Gaza has become both fragile and fierce — a paradox shaped by constraint. These children grow in the cracks of a system that should have broken them, and instead, they flower. They read by lanterns when power fails; they study under tarpaulin tents turned into classrooms; they play football in alleys shadowed by drones.

During one of Layla's storytelling nights, a boy raises his hand. "Miss," he asks, "when I grow up, can I be a doctor and a fighter?" She pauses before answering. "You can heal, and that will be your fight."

Outside, the generator hums. The sky trembles with the distant echo of planes. But inside the room, the children sit cross-legged, wrapped in the fragile armour of imagination. Their crayons glide across paper: homes with gardens, skies without checkpoints, oceans open and infinite. They are drawing not what is, but what could be — and in that act, they redefine reality itself.

Meanwhile, far beyond Gaza's borders, the world scrolls through their stories in headlines and hashtags. In Europe, protests call for ceasefires. In the United States, college students hang banners reading "Let Gaza Live." In South Africa, the government files a case at the International Court of Justice, echoing the call for accountability. And in cities like London, Jakarta, and São Paulo, children their age hold kites painted with olive branches.

It is a strange symmetry — one generation under bombardment, another marching in solidarity — all bound by the shared language of hope.

When night falls, Mariam stands by the window. The sea is dark and calm, the horizon dotted with the faint glow of fishing boats. She whispers into the wind, "Can you hear us?"

Perhaps the world does not yet answer. But the waves reply, whispering back against the stones — steady, endless, patient.

Omar joins her, wrapping an arm around her shoulders. "You know," he says, "the sea keeps every secret." She nods. "Then it must be heavy." He smiles, tracing the outline of her small hand against the glass. "That's why we keep giving it songs — so it won't sink."

From the rooftops, the call to prayer rises, layered and echoing. Somewhere, a generator sputters to silence. Somewhere else, a newborn cries. The city breathes in rhythm again — wounded, beautiful, unbroken.

For these children, the future is not promised. But neither is it denied.

They will grow into engineers who design light grids powered by the sun, into writers who translate their pain into poems, into teachers who rebuild more than classrooms. They will carry the memory of this time not as a burden, but as blueprint — proof that life, even besieged, can still reach upward. And when the world finally learns to listen, it will discover that Gaza's children have already been writing its moral memory — one drawing, one story, one heartbeat at a time.

As Layla writes in her journal that night: "They have seen the worst of us, and they still believe in the best of us. That is what it means to be human."

Global Contrast 2024

While Mariam writes in the journal by candlelight, the rest of the world scrolls past her city on glowing screens. Outside her window, the sky hums with drones and the scent of sea salt; inside, her candle flickers, throwing a trembling halo of gold over her notebook. Each letter she writes leans slightly to the right — small, careful, deliberate, as if climbing toward the light itself.

Beyond Gaza's borders, the rhythm of life moves at another speed.

In Europe, children return to classrooms filled with daylight and laughter, their backpacks heavy with books instead of bottled water. Smartboards blink to life. Teachers write equations on spotless whiteboards. No one flinches at the sound of planes. Their futures are scheduled, timetabled, assumed.

In Tokyo and New York, drones glide between skyscrapers delivering coffee and parcels, their hum mistaken for convenience — not fear. Neon lights bathe the streets. Screens advertise new gadgets, new seasons, new beginnings.

In Dubai, a tower pierces the clouds, illuminated like a promise. In California, billionaires launch rockets into the sky, chasing new planets while Gaza's children count the seconds between airstrikes, learning the arithmetic of survival instead of space.

In one world, light is progress. In another, it's fire. And yet, across those same digital pathways — through broken Wi-Fi, proxy servers, and flickering connections — Mariam's drawings begin to travel. Her sketches of kites, olive trees, and suns drift through timelines and newsfeeds. Huda's poems, handwritten on torn paper and photographed on a cracked phone, find readers in Berlin, Jakarta, and Santiago.

A teacher in Dublin prints Mariam's drawing for her students. A journalist in Nairobi quotes Huda's line — "We grow where we are not allowed to." — in an article about resilience. On social media, their names appear beneath hashtags that pulse through the world's collective conscience.

Each upload from Gaza is a small defiance of silence — a message smuggled through pixels. Every share, every translation, becomes a kind of rescue.

The candle on Mariam's desk burns lower, its wax pooling like memory. She looks at the glow of her tablet — the only screen she owns — and watches the tiny "upload complete" icon blink. Somewhere, far beyond the siege, her picture of the sea appears on another screen, in another time zone, in another life.

For a moment, the world sees her city not as a war zone, but as a place where a child still dares to draw the horizon. And though no rocket has ever left Gaza's soil, her drawing travels farther than any spacecraft — carrying with it the unbreakable truth that imagination has no border.

1.8 CHAPTER 7 — EDUCATION INTERRUPTED: CHILDREN AND THE LOST SCHOOL YEARS

"They send us food so we will not starve,
but never the freedom that would let us feed ourselves."
— Community leader, Gaza City, 2021

Part 1 – Boxes with Flags

After every war, the aid trucks come — long convoys groaning over shattered asphalt, their engines coughing dust like old men clearing their throats. The roads shimmer with heat and diesel, lined with people waiting in the haze. On the trailers, bright flags flap against the wind: blue for the UN, red for the Red Cross, green for Gulf charities, white for European donors.

Children run barefoot alongside the trucks, waving, laughing, calling out, "They've come! They've come!" Their joy rises above the engines, fragile but contagious. To them, the flags mean something good is arriving — rice, milk, sugar, or maybe a toy tucked inside by a kind stranger. To the adults, the sight means survival for another week — and the silent reminder that even hope now comes with customs stamps.

The trucks carry sacks of flour stacked like sandbags, cartons of powdered milk, and something less visible — the faint perfume of foreign generosity, mixed with the sourness of dependency. For a few brief hours, Gaza feels remembered. Cameras flash, journalists take notes, and the dust settles like applause. Then the trucks leave, and the silence returns.

At the port warehouse, Omar stands among rows of crates stamped with acronyms — UNRWA, WFP, Qatar Relief, ECHO. The place smells of burlap, oil, and saltwater. He checks names on lists printed in fading ink, his pen smudging against sweat and dust. Each parcel — rice, oil, lentils, tinned meat — will feed one family for fourteen days, if stretched carefully.

He marks familiar names: widows, teachers, carpenters without jobs. Every name is a story, every number a quiet confession of need. "They call this relief," he mutters to a volunteer, "but it feels more like a rope — and it frays a little more each month."

Nearby, a child tries to lift a sack heavier than himself. Omar bends down to help. "Careful," he says. The boy grins, his face streaked with dust. "I'm strong," he insists. Omar smiles faintly. Strength is the only inheritance Gaza can guarantee its children, he thinks.

That evening, Layla unpacks the day's supplies on their kitchen table: two tins of chickpeas, one bag of flour, cooking oil, soap, and a leaflet printed in three languages — Arabic, English, French — explaining "nutritional balance." The pamphlet is decorated with cheerful fruits no one in Gaza has seen fresh in months.

She runs her fingers over the foreign letters, the careful words of compassion printed far away. The candlelight flickers across her face as she whispers, "We are grateful. But one day, I want to buy our food again — not just receive it."

Omar nods, his eyes on their daughter. At the corner of the table, Mariam sits beside the boxes, practicing her spelling. Her small fingers move slowly over the page.

In her notebook, beneath a smudge of flour, she writes three words in careful English:

Food. Family. Freedom.

Layla leans over her shoulder and smiles softly. "That's the right order," she says. And outside, another aid truck rumbles past in the dark — its engine fading like an echo of kindness that never quite reaches home.

Part 2 – The Bureaucracy of Mercy

To rebuild in Gaza is to drown in paper before touching a single brick.

Every step of reconstruction — every sack of cement, every pane of glass, every nail — must travel through a labyrinth of approvals. Each form bears multiple stamps, each signature another checkpoint. Permits are reviewed by COGAT (the Coordination of Government Activities in the Territories), verified by UN monitors, and logged into distant databases in Geneva, Brussels, or Tel Aviv.

A single shipment of building materials can take months to clear. Cement meant for homes sits under tarps at the border until it clumps into stone. By the time authorization arrives, roofs have collapsed again under rain.

In one of those dim government offices, Omar waits his turn. The room smells of sweat, paper, and stale coffee. A fluorescent light above flickers, buzzing like a trapped insect. The clerk — a young man in an ill-fitting vest — scrolls through endless spreadsheets, squinting at names, coordinates, and funding codes. His tone is polite but hollow.

"Your request is complete," he says without looking up. "But funds are pending. Maybe after the next donor conference."

Omar exhales. "And when is that?" The clerk shrugs, a gesture that could mean tomorrow or never.

Outside, the air is hot and metallic, carrying the faint hum of drones. Across the street, a billboard flaps against a half-standing wall, its slogan in English and Arabic:

"International Reconstruction Summit — Building Peace Together."

Below it, barefoot children play among rubble. None of the families whose names appear in the spreadsheets will ever be invited to that summit.

Omar walks home through streets lined with empty window frames — houses that breathe through holes where glass should be. A donkey cart rattles past, loaded with broken concrete for reuse. Above him, the night sky glows faintly with the lights of surveillance drones, tracing pale arcs across the horizon.

He pauses, looking up. The machines blink like artificial stars — watching, recording, deciding. For a moment, he wonders if the data they collect includes the shape of a man still waiting for permission to rebuild his home.

When he reaches his door, Layla is sitting on the steps, her hands dusted with flour. She looks up at him and smiles wearily.

"No news?" she asks.

"Only forms," he replies.

She nods — not surprised. Then, quietly, she says what everyone in Gaza has come to understand: "Even mercy here needs a permit."

Omar looks out toward the dark horizon, where the drone lights shimmer faintly like false constellations, and thinks: We are rebuilding lives on borrowed approvals.

Part 3 – The Business of Need

Aid feeds Gaza — but it also cages it in dependency. More than 70 percent of households rely on humanitarian assistance, according to UNRWA and World Bank estimates. The economy, strangled by blockade and unemployment, has become a delicate machine powered by two opposing forces: charity and ingenuity.

In the open-air market near Shati Camp, the air hums with barter and survival. The smell of cumin, diesel, and sea wind mixes with the rustle of plastic bags. Vendors shout prices above the drone of generators, their voices half-singing, half-pleading. Layla walks between the stalls, her sandals crunching over broken concrete and spilled grain.

She stops at a table stacked with cooking oil bottles stamped in bold letters: "NOT FOR SALE – HUMANITARIAN AID." The words glare like a secret spoken too loudly.

"Is this legal?" she asks the vendor, a thin man with weary eyes. He wipes sweat from his brow and shrugs. "Legal?" he repeats, almost amused. "Maybe not. But my children eat tonight."

Around them, the market breathes a rhythm of quiet defiance. Women trade lentils for sugar, soap for onions. Men repack flour from UN sacks into smaller bags to sell by the kilo. Teenagers push carts loaded with rice through narrow alleys, shouting, "Blessings! Fresh aid!" as if the goods were harvest from their own soil.

Corruption seeps in at the edges — a permit hurried through with a bribe; a warehouse emptied before the records match the cargo. But alongside it, compassion thrives just as stubbornly. Neighbours share bread baked from aid flour. Families rotate whose generator runs during the night, so everyone gets a few hours of light.

In one corner, an old man sells tiny bouquets of jasmine. "I don't grow food," he says, "but I grow hope." The flowers wilt by noon, but every morning he brings more.

Omar watches a group of boys lifting boxes for a shopkeeper, their laughter echoing down the street. "They should be in school," he says.

"They are," Layla answers quietly. "Just not the kind that gives diplomas."

That night, as she sorts the day's rations by candlelight, Layla opens her journal. Her handwriting trembles slightly with fatigue: "We trade in kindness because it's the only currency that doesn't lose value. Here, even the poor find ways to give — and that's our richest economy."

Outside, the market lights fade one by one as generators die. The silence that follows smells faintly of smoke and soap — and something else, too: the fragile dignity of a people surviving on what the world calls aid, but what they call endurance.

Part 4 – Faith and Foreign Hands

Fridays bring a different kind of aid — the kind that comes not from ministries or agencies, but from faith and neighbourly grace.

At the mosque, sunlight falls through the lattice windows in thin golden lines. Plastic barrels at the entrance overflow with coins and crumpled bills — small offerings wrapped in big prayers. The imam's voice rises, warm and steady, echoing through the courtyard: "Whoever feeds one soul keeps hope alive for all."

The worshippers bow, rows of weary men whose pockets carry more faith than money. After the sermon, they stay behind to sweep the floors, sort the donations, and whisper blessings for unseen families.

Across town, Layla sits with the women's charity committee in a cool, shadowed room that smells faintly of jasmine tea and paper. Their table is covered in envelopes, grocery lists, and folded letters written in careful Arabic script: A widow in need of milk. A student needing bus fare. A newborn without formula.

They pack rice, flour, and sugar into plain brown bags, marking each one with a red thread to remember where it must go. When the streets quiet at dusk, the women move like shadows — leaving envelopes under doors, bags on steps, fruit baskets by windows.

"We call it invisible charity," Layla explains. "Because dignity should travel with the food."

No names are spoken, no photos taken. The help comes like morning light — quietly, faithfully, without witnesses.

Meanwhile, foreign NGOs move through Gaza's edges like tides — arriving with banners and briefings, departing when budgets dry up. Some stay long enough to learn the smell of seaweed and diesel, the way children wave at every white jeep, the rhythm of prayer between blackouts. Others leave as quickly as they came, their promises lost to policy shifts and press releases.

Omar, who has worked beside many, has learned to measure sincerity not by words but by footprints. "If they walk our streets," he says, "if their shoes collect our dust, they care."

That night, after Mariam has fallen asleep, Layla opens her worn notebook and writes by candlelight — a small act of record-keeping against forgetfulness. "Today: one widow's roof repaired with borrowed nails. One scholarship approved after five months of waiting. One baby born safely with donated medicine." She pauses, listening to the hum of the generator outside, then adds a final line: "Each small mercy is a thread in the fabric of survival — and together, they keep this city from unravelling."

Outside, the muezzin's final call drifts through the night air, mingling with the sea breeze and the distant murmur of generators. For a moment, Gaza breathes — fragile, faithful, and still full of unseen hands that hold it together.

Part 5 – Hope in Small Projects

Amid endless forms, missing permits, and waiting lists that never seem to move, small miracles still bloom.

In a vacant lot once filled with rubble, a youth group plants a garden. The soil is poor, the air thick with dust, yet green dares to return. They rig an irrigation system from cracked pipes and an old FAO donation, coaxing water through with laughter and trial. Between the ruins, mint, basil, and cherry tomatoes push through the ground, their scent sharp and clean — a perfume of defiance.

Children arrive with plastic bottles, watering the rows as if baptizing the earth. Their feet leave tiny prints in the dust, and when the first sprouts appear, they clap as though witnessing a resurrection.

Layla visits often, kneeling beside the smallest plants. "This one looks thirsty," she says, her fingers brushing the leaves. Omar smiles from behind the fence, holding a bucket of water. "Everything here is thirsty," he answers. "But look — still, it grows."

Not far away, another miracle hums quietly under a tin roof — Layla's sewing cooperative. Once a corner room with one machine and two women, it now employs twenty. The air smells of fabric, starch, and warm electricity from the solar lamps that power their work.

The women sit shoulder to shoulder, their fingers dancing over cloth. They stitch school uniforms, prayer dresses, and tote bags emblazoned with careful embroidery:

Made in Gaza — With Hope.

The rhythm of the sewing machines becomes a kind of music — steady, pulsing, alive. Half of their products sell locally, carried by market stalls and teachers who wear them proudly. The rest travel beyond the blockade, sold through an online store run by volunteers in London.

When the first digital payment arrives, the women gather around Layla's phone as the screen glows faintly blue. For a moment, it feels like a window opening. Someone shouts, "It worked!" and laughter bursts from the room like sunlight through dust.

They dance to the hum of the generator, their shadows moving across the cracked walls.

Omar teases from the doorway, "So you're all businesswomen now?" Layla wipes a thread of sweat from her cheek and grins. "No. Builders — just like you. Only our bricks are made of thread."

Outside, the evening call to prayer rises, mingling with their laughter and the scent of new cloth. For a heartbeat, Gaza feels mended — seam by seam, stitch by stitch. The city exhales. Hope, it seems, does not always arrive in convoys or contracts.

Sometimes it's delivered by hand, wrapped in fabric, carried by women who refuse to let their world unravel.

Part 6 – Political Games and Donor Fatigue

By 2024, the word conference had lost its meaning. It echoed like a ritual prayer said too often, believed too little. Across Gaza, people watched donor summits on small, flickering screens powered by car batteries. Air-conditioned halls in Cairo, Doha, and Brussels gleamed with crystal water bottles and polished speeches. World leaders spoke of "reconstruction," "a path to peace," and "a brighter Gaza."

Meanwhile, in Beit Hanoun, mothers still cooked lentils over wood fires, and children studied by the light of kerosene lamps.

According to OCHA, less than half of the billions pledged after previous wars ever reached the Strip. The rest dissolved into red tape, rerouted budgets, and forgotten promises. Each year brought new commitments, new press photos — and the same silence once the cameras turned away.

Omar listened to one of these conferences on his old radio while repairing his neighbour's roof. The voice of a foreign minister crackled through the static: "We must rebuild hope." Omar tightened a nail with his bare hand and muttered, "They talk like builders, but they've never carried a brick." Layla, passing him a piece of wood, smiled without humour. "Maybe they fear we'll build something stronger than pity."

Inside the Strip, the real battles were fought not with bombs, but with paper and power.

Ministries argued over who would control the reconstruction funds. NGOs competed for access. Permits vanished between checkpoints. Cement shipments disappeared into the maze of approvals, resurfacing weeks later — lighter, smaller, and more expensive.

A man waiting for his house to be rebuilt called it "the politics of waiting." Every delay became another form of siege. At the local market, Layla overheard a shopkeeper joke, "They send cement with one hand and bureaucracy with the other." The laughter was brief, edged with exhaustion.

Meanwhile, families patched their walls with cardboard, tin, and prayer. Children painted murals over cracked plaster — suns, flowers, Arabic verses — as if colour could substitute for stability. The streets smelled of dust, diesel, and patience.

Foreign correspondents came, filmed the ruins, and left before nightfall. Their footage — carefully edited, subtitled, and scored with sombre music — reached Europe faster than a single bag of cement ever would.

When the power returned that evening for an hour, Layla sat by the window scrolling through her phone, watching the same speeches replayed on social media. "Do they ever see what we see?" she asked softly.

Omar shook his head, eyes on the unfinished roofline against the sunset. "They don't see us," he said. "They see a project." Outside, the generator hummed to life again, drowning the static of the radio. In the glow of the single bulb, Layla picked up her pen and wrote in her journal: "We build from the scraps of their promises. And still, somehow, the walls rise."

Part 7 – Local Resilience

When the world's help slows, Gaza's people create their own. Innovation grows here like a weed through cracks in the concrete — stubborn, uninvited, unstoppable.

Local engineers salvage wires and scrap metal from destroyed workshops, fashioning solar panels out of broken mirrors and car batteries. Under roofs patched with tarpaulins, young technicians solder circuits that flicker back to life. They joke that sunlight is Gaza's only borderless import.

In the farmlands of Khan Younis, farmers purify brackish water by layering sand, charcoal, and crushed limestone inside oil drums. They harvest tomatoes and spinach in soil that still smells faintly of salt and ash. "We water with hope," one farmer laughs, "because we have little else."

In the city, balconies have become vertical gardens. Plastic buckets hang from rebar rods, filled with mint, parsley, and basil. The scent travels down the narrow alleys, softening the smell of diesel and sea wind. Layla runs her hand along the leaves, proud of the small forest blooming between bullet holes.

Her cooperative, once a sewing circle, now partners with a youth-led start-up to recycle plastic waste into paving tiles. The work is messy — heat, fumes, and long hours — but the first path they lay leads from the street to the local school. Children walk barefoot across it, tracing their initials in the wet surface before it hardens.

Omar, watching from the fence, grins. "If the world won't send us roads," he says, "we'll make our own."

Faith groups, scout clubs, and students knit together a web of mutual aid that no blockade can break. In one neighbourhood, a bakery powered by a donated generator feeds two hundred families daily. In another, IT graduates design an app connecting leftover restaurant food to local shelters — the first of its kind in Gaza.

During Ramadan, Layla joins volunteers delivering food parcels to widows and orphans. They move from door to door with quiet dignity — no banners, no cameras, only compassion. At one home, an elderly woman named Aisha opens her door, her hands trembling with age. When Layla offers her a parcel of flour, rice, and sugar, Aisha takes the sugar packet and gently places it back in the bag. "Give it to someone who needs it more," she says. Layla insists, but Aisha smiles — a slow, knowing smile that feels centuries old "Child," she says softly, "generosity is the only wealth we still own."

Layla stands at the doorway, unable to speak. The air smells of bread baking somewhere nearby, and in the distance, the muezzin's call rises over the hum of generators. In that moment, she feels something larger than despair — a quiet, defiant grace. Because in Gaza, even survival becomes an art form — one built not on aid or politics, but on the patient, ordinary courage of people who refuse to vanish.

Part 8 – Closing Reflections: What Help Means

On a warm evening, the power lasts longer than usual — a rare, golden gift.

The fan hums softly; the bulbs glow without flicker. From their balcony, Omar and Layla watch the neighbourhood pulse back to life.

Children play between half-rebuilt houses, chasing a ball through the dust. Someone's radio plays an old love song. The smell of fresh bread and diesel smoke drifts up from Fatima's oven, blending into the air like memory and survival intertwined.

The muezzin's call rises from the nearby mosque, merging with the rhythm of laughter below — a strange harmony of prayer and play that feels, for a heartbeat, like peace.

Omar leans on the balcony rail, eyes tracing the sunset bleeding over the sea — orange melting into grey, a horizon marked by both beauty and blockade. "Sometimes," he says softly, "I wonder if aid saves us — or just keeps us waiting."

Layla doesn't answer right away. She watches Mariam skip between puddles below, her braids bouncing, her laughter echoing through the narrow street. Then she takes Omar's hand, their fingers rough from work, warm from persistence.

"Both," she says finally. "But while we wait, we still live. That part — no one can give or take."

They sit together in silence, the kind that feels earned. The call to prayer fades, replaced by the rustle of the sea breeze against the clotheslines.

They talk quietly about the future — about teaching Mariam to grow food, to fix what breaks, to share before asking, to believe in people more than promises. "She must know the world is bigger than its borders," Layla says.

Omar looks toward the horizon, where the last aid trucks had disappeared days before, leaving only the long road and the whisper of engines fading into the dunes. "Maybe real help," he murmurs, "is when we stop needing boxes with flags."

Later that night, by candlelight, Layla opens her worn notebook and writes:

They send us food, but we share it.

They send us money, but we build with it.

They send us hope, but we already had our own.

When the generator finally clicks off, the city falls into darkness — deep, enveloping, familiar. But above it, the stars ignite, scattering light across the sky. They shine without logos, without borders, without conditions.

Layla looks up and whispers to Mariam, now half-asleep beside her: "See, habibti — even the stars don't belong to anyone." And in that quiet, Gaza breathes — not as a place defined by crisis, but as a people who endure, who rebuild, who love in the dark and still reach for the light. Because real help is not what arrives in trucks. It is what remains when the trucks are gone.

1.9 CHAPTER 8 – THE SEA BETWEEN US: LOVE, LOSS, AND THE DREAM OF LEAVING

"Every tide asks the same question: will you cross me or stay?"
— Fisherman's proverb, Gaza 2022

Part 1 – The Call of the Sea

The sea has always been Gaza's only horizon — its only window and its oldest wound.

It breathes just beyond the city's edge, a shifting line between blue and grey, between what is possible and what is forbidden.

From their rooftop in Gaza City, Layla and Omar can just glimpse it — a narrow ribbon of shimmer framed by broken rooftops, satellite dishes, and the faint silhouettes of watchtowers. Some mornings, when the wind blows west, the smell of salt drifts inland, weaving through alleys, over laundry lines, and through open windows. It mixes with the scent of diesel from generators and fresh bread from the bakery below — a bittersweet perfume of survival.

To many, that smell is freedom. To others, it's memory. To Layla, it is both.

Before dawn, the fishermen begin their quiet pilgrimage toward the shore.

Their boats — once painted bright turquoise and white — now bear scars of years and bullets. The men push them into the surf with steady, wordless effort. Beyond six nautical miles lies the invisible border patrolled by naval boats. The fishermen know its exact distance not by maps, but by instinct — the horizon changes colour, by the feeling in the air when danger begins.

Beyond that line, warning shots wait. Arrest waits. Sometimes, death waits.

Still, they go. Hunger is heavier than fear.

In 2021, three young men never came back. Their motor failed just beyond the line. For two days, families waited on the shore, eyes fixed on the horizon that did not answer. When the tide returned, so did the bodies — wrapped in seaweed and nets, like messages that had tried and failed to reach the world. The sea, that year, was both coffin and witness.

Yet the next morning, other fishermen launched their boats again. Children helped push them out, their feet sinking in the cold foam. "May the tide be kind," an old man whispered, crossing himself before casting the net. In Gaza, faith is measured not in prayers, but in the courage to keep going.

Sometimes, at night, when the tide hums through the narrow alleys, Layla stands on the roof and closes her eyes. The sound of the waves reaches her through the dark — steady, eternal, like a heartbeat larger than the city itself. She imagines another coast, not one of exile or escape, but of openness — a place where the horizon isn't patrolled, where boats leave and return without permission, where the sea is just sea, not a border.

She turns to Omar. "If the sea had a voice," she says softly, "it would urge us to keep going."

Omar, sitting beside her with a wrench in his hand and the dust of the day still on his clothes, smiles wearily. "And who will rebuild the walls if we leave?"

His question hangs between them like the last light on the water — fading, unresolved. Layla doesn't answer. She just listens to the tide. Because in Gaza, the question of leaving is older than either of them, older even than the blockade. It is the sound beneath every wave: stay or go, stay, or go — the rhythm of a life caught between endurance and escape.

Part 2 – The Border That Breathes

Leaving Gaza is not a journey; it is a siege of patience — a crossing of time more than distance.

To the north lies Erez Crossing, the iron throat of departure, where concrete walls rise higher than hope. Inside, everything hums: biometric scanners, metal detectors, cameras that see more than eyes should. Travelers move in silence, clutching permits like fragile miracles. Only a handful — humanitarian cases, traders, a few students — pass each month. The rest wait, months, or years, for their names to appear on invisible lists.

To the south, the Rafah Crossing — Gaza's other lung — opens and closes without warning. It is not a gate but a mood: political, unpredictable, alive one week, sealed the next.

When it opens, the queue stretches for kilometres — a human tapestry of exhaustion. Mothers cradle folders of medical papers; students guard scholarship letters like passports to another planet. Fathers balance bags of medicine, documents, and dreams. The waiting area smells of dust, sweat, and anticipation — a perfume of desperation and faith.

123

Omar once accompanied his cousin Khaled to Rafah. They arrived before dawn, their breath visible in the cool air. Around them, hundreds waited — an ocean of suitcases and plastic bags, of whispered prayers and stale bread. Loudspeakers crackled, calling names in groups of twenty. Each name was a heartbeat, each silence, a small death.

Khaled's name never came.

By nightfall, the air shimmered with heat and diesel fumes. Omar watched his cousin's face dry into resignation. His lips cracked; his hands trembled not from anger but from emptiness. When they finally turned back toward Gaza City, the headlights carved through the dust like ghosts returning to a cage. Khaled didn't speak the whole way home.

According to OCHA, fewer than one percent of Gaza's residents receive exit permits each year. Those who do are mostly patients, students, or foreign-aid workers — people who leave for treatment or study, not for escape. Many never return. Their absence becomes another kind of exile, a wound that travels through phone lines and voice notes.

Layla felt it the day her friend Rasha, a nurse, received her scholarship for training in Cairo. For weeks, the two women packed at night by lantern light, folding clothes, and courage in equal measure. On the morning of departure, they stood together at the bus depot, the air thick with diesel and tears.

"I will come back," Rasha promised. "When I can heal without borders."

People clapped quietly — not in celebration, but in reverence for someone who had managed to leave. Yet everyone knew what Layla could not say aloud: borders rarely let love return easily.

As the bus disappeared in a cloud of sand, Layla whispered a prayer into the wind, one carried toward the sea — the same sea that both connects and confines. In Gaza, even farewell is a form of resistance, and even departure is only half a freedom.

Part 3 – The Argument

It began one humid night when the power died mid-cooking. The fridge exhaled a long, final sigh; then silence swallowed the room. The fan stopped turning, and the air thickened, heavy with diesel, sweat, and the metallic scent of heat. Layla waved a notebook over Mariam's flushed face while Omar knelt beside the old generator, its engine coughing in protest.

Outside, the neighbourhood pulsed with the familiar symphony of outages — distant shouts, the whir of private generators, a baby's cry cutting through the dark. Somewhere down the street, someone struck a match; the faint glow of a candle trembled through an open window.

Layla's voice rose softly above the machine's choking hum. "Maybe we should apply for visas," she said, almost to herself. "Just to try." Omar's hands froze on the greasy lever. For a heartbeat, even the generator seemed to pause. "To where?" he asked, turning toward her. "They don't want us anywhere."

She kept fanning Mariam, her tone measured but sharp. "Some families manage. Canada, Türkiye, anywhere with light that stays on — anywhere she can sleep without drones."

Omar wiped oil from his palms with a rag and stood. His face was half in shadow, half in the amber flicker of the candle. "We belong here," he said. "Every brick I lay says my name. Out there, we'd be ghosts again — refugees building someone else's walls." Layla looked at him for a long time, her eyes burning with the quiet rage of someone tired of surviving. "And what about Mariam?" she whispered. "She deserves more than waiting rooms and curfews."

The generator sputtered, coughed, then roared to life, flooding the room with harsh yellow light. For a moment, the noise filled the space where their words might have lived. Neither spoke again. Omar turned away, tightening a bolt that didn't need tightening. Layla held Mariam close, feeling the child's breath steady against her chest. The hum of the machine became the pulse of their unspoken fears — loud, relentless, unresolved.

Later that night, when the generator finally choked silent again, Layla noticed a drawing taped to the wall. It was Mariam's newest picture: a small, uneven boat floating toward a bright sun. On the distant shore stood a little house, its door open, waiting.

At the bottom, in crooked English letters, she had written: Both Home. Layla traced the words with her fingertip. In that moment, she realized their daughter had already crossed the sea — if not in body, then in imagination.

Part 4 – Departures and Remittances

By autumn, the silence that had followed their argument turned into something new — a chorus of departures. Across Gaza, leaving became the season's conversation.

Cafés hummed with rumours and hope.

"Qatar is taking teachers."

"Germany needs nurses."

"Canada will open its doors next year."

Each whisper spread like folklore, passed from phone to phone, street to street — the new currency of possibility.

In the evenings, Omar and Layla would sit on their rooftop, hearing the hum of generators below and the drone of the sea beyond. From every house came stories of someone leaving — a cousin bound for Türkiye, a neighbour accepted into a scholarship in Norway. Even the imam's son, who once led prayers, now sent voice notes from Berlin, describing rain that never smelled of smoke.

Soon, familiar faces began to vanish.

Barbershops hung "Closed" signs that never came down; classrooms lost their brightest students. On cracked phone screens, those who had gone sent back photographs of wide, clean streets and uninterrupted light — streets without checkpoints, nights without buzzing drones.

Yet every message ended the same way: I miss the sea.

Money began to return before people did. Remittances — invisible threads stretched across the Mediterranean — became Gaza's quiet lifeline. By 2024, according to the World Bank, nearly one in five households survived on money sent from abroad. Each transfer arrived like a heartbeat — proof that the outside world still remembered.

Omar accompanied his cousin's wife to a Western Union office near the port. The queue wound out the door, a line of anxious patience. Inside, fluorescent lights flickered, and fans spun the scent of dust and sweat.

When her name was called, she stepped forward, received the thin envelope of cash, and stared at it as if it might dissolve in her hands. Tears welled. "Every coin carries distance," she murmured. Omar nodded. He knew — each dollar was a promise sent by someone who could not come home.

That evening, the house was unusually quiet. The generator's hum seemed distant, the sea outside restless. Layla sat before their old computer, its keyboard missing two keys, and opened an online application for a teaching position abroad.

Her certificates, scanned under flickering light, glowed faintly on the screen. She typed her name — Layla Hassan — then paused at the final button: Submit.

Her pulse echoed in her ears, a rhythm like waves breaking against stone. She thought of Mariam asleep in the next room, of Omar's calloused hands, of jasmine on the balcony still struggling to bloom.

Omar entered quietly and stood behind her. His shadow fell over the screen. "You don't need permission to dream," he said softly, his hand resting on her shoulder. "Just don't forget where the dream began."

Layla's finger hovered over the mouse. For a long moment, she looked at the word Submit — at its double meaning — then slowly moved her hand away. The generator flickered. The screen dimmed. She did not press it. Not yet.

Part 5 – Temporary Separation

In November 2024, Omar accepted a short contract with an NGO tasked with rebuilding homes near Rafah, close to the Egyptian border. It meant six months apart — the first real distance between him and Layla since their wedding. He told her it was temporary. But in Gaza, even the word temporary carried uncertainty.

At dawn, the street was still half-asleep. Omar packed his small bag — gloves, a notebook, a tin of coffee, and a framed photo of Layla and Mariam taken on the rooftop the night of the ceasefire. The frame was chipped, the glass slightly cracked, but he wrapped it carefully in his clothes.

Layla watched him fold each item as if it were a part of their home. Before he closed the bag, she tucked in a sprig of dried jasmine from their rooftop garden. "For luck," she whispered. Omar smiled faintly. "In Gaza, luck is just another kind of faith."

When the bus finally pulled away, Layla stood in the doorway, Mariam's hand clasped in hers. The air smelled of dust, bread baking, and diesel from departing vehicles. Around them, the neighbourhood stirred awake — shutters rising, roosters calling, the faint buzz of a generator starting somewhere down the alley. "He'll come back soon," Layla said, forcing her voice steady. Mariam nodded but didn't let go of her hand until the bus vanished from sight.

That night, the house felt enormous in his absence — every creak of the walls a reminder of the missing sound of his laughter. The sea breeze no longer brought comfort; it only carried distance. Communication became another battlefield. Phone lines failed; connections dropped mid-sentence. When a message did arrive, it was short, fragile — a flicker of presence across a failing network: All good. Still building. Miss you.

Sometimes those words arrived hours late, sometimes not at all. On those nights, Layla wrote back anyway, as if her replies could find him through static and air: We watered the jasmine. Mariam asked about the stars. The city is waiting for you.

One night, long after midnight, the phone rang. Omar's voice, thin and trembling through the static, came from somewhere near the border. "I can see the lights from here," he said softly. "They shimmer on the sea — like another city beneath the waves." Layla closed her eyes, imagining it — the illusion of another Gaza reflected in the dark water, untouched, unbroken.

"Maybe one day we'll visit it together," she whispered. He laughed quietly, the sound warm but weary. "Maybe. But for now, I build this one."

After the call ended, Layla sat for a long time beside the silent phone. The hum of the generator had stopped, leaving only the faint echo of waves and her daughter's breathing from the next room.

Each night, Mariam marked her father's absence on a paper calendar, drawing a small seashell for every day he was gone. "One for every sunrise Baba miss," she said. The shells began as neat rows but soon covered the entire page, overlapping like waves on a shore.

1.10 CHAPTER 9 — ROMANCE, RESILIENCE: HUMAN LIGHT IN DARK TIMES

"Even in a land that forgets to sleep, love still dreams."

Part 1 — The Weight of Another Year

The year 2025 arrived in Gaza without fireworks or celebration — only the low, familiar hum of drones circling above the Mediterranean. The air was cold and damp; the kind of chill that seeps into walls already cracked by years of siege.

Electricity came for two hours a day, flickering like an unreliable heartbeat. Water flowed from the taps every three days — thin, brown, and metallic. Still, the city stirred each morning, as it always did, with the sound of kettles, pigeons, and prayer.

When Omar finally returned, his hands were blistered, his eyes lined with fatigue. But as he entered the courtyard, Mariam ran to him, clutching the shell-covered calendar. "Look, Baba," she said, holding it up like a map. "You came back before I ran out of days." Omar lifted her into his arms. Layla stood in the doorway, the jasmine blooming again behind her. For a moment, the three of them stood framed in the soft morning light — reunited, fragile, but whole.

It was neither departure nor arrival — just the quiet rhythm of a people who refuse to sink. For Gaza — for Layla and Omar, for every fisherman who sails at dawn, for every mother who teaches by candlelight, for every child who dares to dream beneath the hum of drones — the sea is no longer only a border. It is a mirror. A witness. A promise that even behind walls, some souls will always reach for the horizon.

Layla and Omar had been married seventeen years now. Their daughter, Mariam, nearly sixteen, was growing fast — tall, sharp-eyed, her laughter quick but fleeting. She was old enough to understand irony, yet young enough to still believe in miracles.

They lived in a small apartment on Al-Rimal Street, repaired after the 2021 bombing with cement donated by the UNDP Reconstruction Programme. The walls were freshly painted a shade of soft sky blue — an act of defiance disguised as decoration, a stubborn wish for calm seas.

Outside, Gaza pulsed with contradiction: rubble beside bakeries, wedding songs beside air-raid sirens. Children walked to school past piles of broken stone, while shopkeepers swept their doorsteps as though cleanliness itself could summon normalcy.

Each morning, Layla rose before sunrise. She boiled tea on a gas burner, guarding every drop of fuel like treasure. Omar joined her on the balcony, where pigeons nested in the window frame. "It's our alarm clock," he joked, his breath clouding in the freezing air. But his smile rarely reached his eyes.

The news reached them through the cracked screen of Layla's phone. Headlines from foreign networks scrolled in careful language: "Renewed escalation," "humanitarian crisis," "calls for restraint." Words that softened the jagged edges of reality — the sound of walls collapsing, the cries that followed, the silence that settled after.

The United Nations Office for the Coordination of Humanitarian Affairs (OCHA) reported that more than 80% of Gaza's population faced catastrophic or emergency food insecurity. Hospitals operated at less than 30% capacity, their wards dimly lit by backup generators. UNRWA warned that it was running out of funds. Even aid had become political, shipments delayed for weeks at checkpoints over diplomatic disputes. And yet — amid all this, life went on.

Layla kneaded dough for bread, her hands dusted with flour. Omar stood outside, polishing a solar oven he'd built from broken mirrors and scrap metal. "We'll warm ourselves with ingenuity," he said with a grin that almost held light. It wasn't a joke — in Gaza, survival was not only endurance; it was artistry.

At night, when the lights died again, the reflection of their small lamp shimmered across the blue walls — fragile, flickering, but steady. Outside, the sea whispered its old refrain through the wind: We're still here.

Part 2 — Love Letters in the Rubble

A week after Omar's return, the air in their apartment still carried the scent of plaster, salt, and something tender that had no name. Life was slowly remembering its rhythm — the kettle's whistle, the murmur of the radio, the quiet sound of two people breathing under the same roof again.

One afternoon, while rearranging a box of old clothes near the stairwell, Layla found a faded bundle tied with frayed string. The envelopes were creased and salt-stained, edges curled from the dampness of winter. For a moment, she didn't recognize them. Then she saw his handwriting — deliberate, patient, the same way he built walls — and her breath caught.

They were the letters Omar had sent during his six months away, when the phone network often collapsed and words had to travel by drivers, aid workers, and luck. Some had arrived after weeks, some never at all. Now, they sat in her hands like a time she had tried not to remember.

That evening, when the light failed again, she lit a candle and unfolded the first one. Omar sat beside her, his arm in quiet contact with hers. The paper smelled faintly of dust and diesel. His voice came softly, almost embarrassed, as she read aloud the words he had once written: "My love, today the sea was too quiet. The men say it's bad luck when it doesn't move. I think it just holds its breath until we come home."

Layla's eyes shimmered. She turned to another letter, his words trembling on the page. "If the sky falls, I will hold up the horizon with my hands for you." She looked at him across the candlelight. "You really wrote that," she said, half-laughing through her tears. "You and your impossible promises." Omar smiled, a slow, weary smile. "I had to believe my hands could do something more than build walls. Writing to you kept them steady."

Outside, the wind rattled the shutters; the candle flame bent and straightened again. Layla touched the stack of letters, their edges dark with travel. "How did we manage it?" she asked quietly. "All those months apart — the silence, the waiting? He leaned back, watching the flame dance in her eyes. "We didn't manage it," he said. "We endured it. There's a difference." She nodded. "And yet we're here." Omar reached for her hand, rough palm against soft skin. "Maybe love," he murmured, "is the only architecture that survives collapse. We just kept building in the dark." Layla smiled faintly, brushing a thumb along the folded letters. "Then we must be the last builders standing."

They sat together, reading until the candle burned low — his words returning to their source, her laughter threading through the silences between sentences. When the wick finally died, they remained in the dark, holding hands, listening to the hum of the sea through the open window — steady, patient, like a pulse older than their sorrow.

In Gaza, even the act of remembering is defiance. Every letter kept, every word read aloud, is another way of saying: we were strong enough to wait.

Part 3 — The Famine Line

By July 2025, Gaza had learned a new kind of hunger — one that gnawed not only at stomachs but at patience itself. The World Food Programme called it "one step from famine." On the ground, it felt closer than that.

The wheat fields along the border lay untended, their soil cracked like old skin. Fishing was still limited to six nautical miles — a line drawn on the sea like a wound that refused to close.

Diesel was scarcer than medicine. Without it, bakeries fell silent, their chimneys cold, their windows smeared with flour that no one had the strength to wash away. Even the air felt thinner, as if the blockade had begun to starve the sky.

Layla spent her mornings at the community kitchen run by the Red Crescent. Beneath a patchwork canopy of plastic sheets, women stirred vast pots of lentils and rice, the steam rising like incense. The clatter of ladles mixed with murmured prayers, the rhythm of necessity.

"Measure by love, not by volume," Layla told Mariam, who stood beside her with sleeves rolled, face damp with heat and determination. Each bowl they filled felt like a small victory — an act of care in a world that had forgotten tenderness.

At the far end of the tent, an old woman whispered blessings over the food. "For every spoonful," she said, "may a heart stay steady. "And so, they stirred, whispered, served — feeding not only hunger, but the fragile idea of tomorrow.

Meanwhile, Omar worked with a group of volunteers repairing broken water tanks across the neighbourhoods. He moved between rooftops with his toolkit and a limp that still reminded him of his months in Rafah. The sun burned against the corrugated metal; the heat shimmered above the city like a fever.

At noon, the sound of drones drifted overhead — a low, metallic hum that never left. Omar paused, squinting at the sky. "Even water," he said to the young men beside him, "has become a border." Then, quieter: "We can't drink politics." They laughed, tired and proud, and went back to work — tightening bolts, sealing cracks, coaxing rusted pipes into endurance.

By evening, the streets glowed orange in the dust. Layla returned home with the smell of lentils in her clothes; Omar arrived later, his hands smelling of tar and metal.

They ate together by candlelight — half a loaf between them, a bowl of soup, and silence thick with fatigue. But when Mariam read aloud from her notebook — a blog post she'd drafted titled "Hunger Doesn't Speak, It Waits" — both parents smiled faintly, their pride a quiet warmth.

That same week, the UN Human Rights Council released its report: "Systemic collapse of civilian infrastructure... collective punishment through siege." The words reached them through the static of the radio — careful, polished, distant.

Omar looked up from his notebook, where he had been sketching plans for a community water system. His voice was low. "The world scrolls past us," he said, almost to himself.

Layla wiped her hands on a towel, her eyes catching the last flicker of the candlelight. "Then we'll write long enough for them to stop," she answered.

Outside, a thin crescent moon hung over the city — pale and watchful. In its light, the rooftops gleamed faintly, like open palms holding on to what little they could. And in one of those homes, between hunger and hope, a family shared bread and silence — and called it love.

Part 4 — The Night of the Lanterns

By late summer, the city had almost forgotten what steady light looked like.

Power came for an hour, then vanished again, leaving behind a silence that hummed with fatigue. The blackout stretched into its fifth consecutive night — a darkness so complete it seemed to swallow sound. So, the neighbourhood decided to fight it the only way they knew how: with light made by hand.

Layla was the first to suggest it. "If the grid won't shine," she said, "we will." She gathered the neighbours on the rooftop, passing around old jars, candle stubs, and string. Children dipped brushes into leftover watercolours, painting the glass in trembling strokes — pomegranate red, sea green, sky blue. Every colour felt like defiance.

By sunset, the rooftop looked like a workshop of hope. Mariam filled the jars with small candles scavenged from the mosque storeroom; Omar climbed the railing, tying the glowing jars to laundry lines that stretched between rooftops. The glass trembled gently in the evening wind, catching the last rays of the dying sun.

When the power finally failed — when the last bulb blinked and the neighbourhood dropped into black — the lanterns came

137

alive. Hundreds of small flames swayed above the ruins, reflected in puddles and window glass, turning the battered skyline into a constellation.

From one rooftop to another, voices rose: laughter, murmured prayers, songs too soft to identify. Omar stood beside Layla and read aloud, his voice steady against the wind: "We love life whenever we can." — Mahmoud Darwish

Layla smiled and echoed softly, "Whenever we can." Then she leaned over and kissed his cheek — a brief, radiant moment, bright as the jar light around them.

Later that night, Mariam sat beside her, eyes reflecting the firelight. "Mama," she asked, "why do we make lanterns when the world could just give us light?" Layla looked at Omar. He gathered Mariam into his arms, his voice calm and certain. "Because" he said, "light we make ourselves can't be taken away."

The wind rose, carrying the warm scent of wax and salt. From the rooftops, the city seemed to float — a small island of moving light adrift in a sea of darkness. And for one fragile, miraculous night, Gaza glowed — not with electricity, but with the power of its own hands.

Part 5 — The Long Summer

By July 2025, Gaza felt like a furnace sealed from the inside. The temperature climbed above forty degrees, and the air shimmered with dust so fine it clung to the skin like salt. The streets were quiet during daylight — only the hum of flies, the distant grind of generators, and the occasional bark of a dog too tired to move.

Electricity came for an hour, sometimes two, but never when it was needed. People learned to listen for the sudden click of current — the cue to rush, to charge phones, run washing machines, pump water, and bake bread all at once before darkness reclaimed everything.

When the power died, the city sighed — a long exhale of heat and fatigue.

Water came every three days, but even then, it was thick with salt. Layla kept a small filter by the sink, rinsing it again until her fingers pruned. She boiled what she could for tea, saving the clear half for drinking and the rest for cleaning.

Mariam helped carry buckets from the communal tank at the end of the street, her small arms trembling under the weight. Sometimes, the water was so hot from sitting in black pipes all day that it steamed in the cups.

Omar spent his days on rebuilding sites near Khan Younis, working with a UNDP Cash-for-Work crew patching roofs and repairing wells. He travelled there on the back of a truck at dawn with other men — engineers, teachers, carpenters — all turned labourers by blockade and survival.

The pay was small, but steady. Six dollars for a day under the sun. Enough for lentils, gas, and bread.

He wrapped his hands in torn cloth to keep the tools from reopening old blisters.

"They say we're rebuilding Gaza," he told Layla one evening, sitting by the open window. "But really, Gaza rebuilds us. It keeps us from breaking."

At home, Layla taught in what had once been their living room — now a classroom for eight neighbourhood children. They came barefoot, clutching worn notebooks, their pencils gnawed to stubs. She used old cereal boxes as writing boards and chalk scavenged from a demolished school.

When the heat grew unbearable, she read stories aloud instead — tales of sea turtles, of cities with rivers that never ran dry. The children listened, half-dreaming, until the sound of a drone above reminded them where they were.

By night, the city glowed faintly with the scattered lights of solar lanterns and phone screens. The power plant had long gone silent, so families gathered on rooftops to catch the sea breeze.

Layla and Omar sat there too, Mariam between them, the sky above full of static stars. Below, the sea murmured its old refrain — sometimes gentle, sometimes angry, always nearby.

A rumour spread that the desalination plant in the north might close entirely. Another said more fuel was coming through Egypt. Hope and dread mingled like humidity — thick, inescapable.

One night, as the fan sputtered on their solar battery, Layla whispered, "If love had a scent, it would be salt and smoke."

Omar smiled faintly, tracing the blistered edge of his palm. "Then this whole place is made of love," he said.

They both laughed — not because it was funny, but because laughter was the only thing that didn't run out.

And outside, in the sleepless heat, Gaza breathed — slow, shallow, but alive.

Each rebuilt wall, each bucket of water, each shared meal was an act of defiance in a world that had grown too used to their endurance.

The long summer stretched on — shimmering, blistered, and human — another chapter in a place that refused to vanish.

Part 6 — The Letter in the Rubble

In August, the air was still heavy with the scent of concrete dust and sea salt. Gaza's summer heat pressed down like a hand that would not lift. Omar joined a group of volunteers clearing debris near the Khan Younis market — once a bustling maze of fruit stalls, spice vendors, and shouts of barter. Now it was quiet except for the scrape of shovels and the occasional cry when something familiar was found: a child's shoe, a prayer bead, a torn photograph.

They worked without machinery; fuel was too scarce. Each brick was moved by hand, each wall dismantled stone by stone. Omar's palms were blistered and raw. But he refused to stop — rebuilding, even in fragments, gave him something solid to stand on when everything else felt like sand.

Just before noon, the call to prayer echoed through the ruins. Omar paused, wiped his forehead, and leaned against a half-standing column. A few men spread their jackets on the dust to pray. As he turned to lift another beam, he heard the groan of shifting concrete — a sound too familiar, too late. The wall collapsed.

The world went white, then silent. When he woke, everything was muted — the ringing in his ears, the shouts fading in and out. Pain bloomed in his leg, sharp and deep. A young boy was kneeling beside him; dust streaked across his face. "Uncle, don't sleep," the boy said, gripping his hand. "They're coming."

He didn't remember the journey to the hospital, only flashes — the smell of diesel, a woman weeping, the siren of an ambulance that wasn't really an ambulance at all but a borrowed truck.

At Al-Quds Hospital, chaos had replaced order. Corridors overflowed with stretchers. The floors were slick with antiseptic and sweat. Doctors moved like ghosts through the half-dark, guided by the light of phones because the power had failed again. The air was filled with the low hum of generators and the faint sound of someone reciting a prayer.

Layla arrived breathless, clutching a bag of water bottles and dates. She pushed through the crowd, calling his name until a nurse grabbed her arm. It was Rasha — older now, her face marked by sleepless years but her eyes still steady. "We saved him," she said, squeezing Layla's hand. "He'll need rest — and patience. And you'll need strength for both."

Omar lay on a cot near the window, his leg encased in plaster, his skin pale beneath the dust. He tried to smile when he saw her. "Don't cry," he murmured. "I just fell into our work again." She laughed through her tears, the kind of laugh that comes from both relief and exhaustion.

That night, when the hallways grew quiet except for the murmuring of patients, Layla sat beside him in the dim light. The room smelled of iodine and candle wax. Outside, the city hummed faintly — generators, waves, the pulse of a place that never truly slept.

On the small table by his bed lay the half-burned letter Mariam had found months ago while they were cleaning the rubble of an old apartment. Its edges were blackened, the ink smudged but still legible in parts. The handwriting belonged to someone long gone — a lover, perhaps, or a parent writing during another war. The words had ended abruptly mid-sentence:

"If you ever find this, know that I was still waiting for—" The rest was ash.

Layla unfolded the letter slowly, smoothing it with her fingers. Then, taking a pen from her bag, she began to write beneath the unfinished line: "We hold up the horizon together now. Even the dust learns our names."

When Omar woke hours later, he saw it swaying gently, half-light, half shadow. He reached for her hand. "You finished someone else's story," he whispered. Layla smiled, brushing a strand of hair from his forehead. "In Gaza," she said softly, "we all finish what others had to stop."

For days afterward, Omar watched the letter whenever he woke. In the mornings, sunlight turned the ink gold; by evening, the salt air had curled its edges. He began to think about the people who had once lived in that ruined apartment — how they too must have loved, built, dreamed, waited. He imagined the writer, whoever they were, sitting by candlelight as he now did, holding faith in the middle of chaos. The thought steadied him.

When he could finally stand with crutches, he asked Rasha to help him to the window. Together they looked out across the courtyard. Dozens of patients had gathered there, their bandages white in the dim light. A boy played an oud made from an old oil can. A girl, perhaps ten years old, balanced a tray of tea glasses, her laughter cutting through the heaviness of the air.

For a moment, Omar felt something shift inside him — not hope exactly, but its shadow, the thing that comes before it: the decision to live again. He turned to Rasha. "It's strange," he said. "Even after all this, the city still feels alive. As if it refuses to believe it's dying." Rasha nodded. "Gaza's like the olive trees," she replied. "Cut them down, and they grow from the roots."

When he was discharged weeks later, Omar returned home on crutches. The apartment still smelled faintly of salt and plaster. Layla had cleared a space near the window for him to sit, facing the sea. Mariam had added her own touch — a small frame holding a copy of the letter, laminated to protect it from the air. Beneath it, she had written in blue pen: "The story continues."

Omar would sit there for hours, watching the horizon. Sometimes he imagined the ghosts of those who had written letters like theirs, floating somewhere above the sea, reading the words that finished their unfinished dreams.

In the quiet moments between pain and recovery, he understood something that no sermon or speech could teach — that survival was not just the absence of death. It was the constant rewriting of what had been destroyed.

He whispered to Layla one night, "I used to think building meant stone and cement. But maybe it's this — letters, promises, the way we keep each other standing." She took his hand and pressed it to her heart. "That's the only foundation that lasts," she said.

Outside, the waves rolled against the shore, and from a nearby rooftop came the sound of children flying kites made from torn plastic bags — bright patches of colour against the greying sky. Omar closed his eyes and listened. Each kite was a message, each flutter a testament.

The wind carried their laughter past the window where the letter hung, across the alleyways, beyond the checkpoints, and into the dark where the world might still be listening.

And though he could not see it, Omar smiled — because somewhere, someone would hear. Because even in rubble, there are stories waiting to be finished.

Because even in silence, there are words still being written.

Outside Gaza, the world was stirring — not with governments, but with people. In London, a river of protestors flowed across Westminster Bridge, their chants echoing between the old stone buildings. Flags of red, green, black, and white rippled like living fire above the crowd. Children rode on their parents' shoulders, holding hand-painted signs that read, "Let Gaza Live" and "Stop the Siege." From the air, the march looked like a single organism breathing — thousands of hearts moving to one rhythm, one plea: Ceasefire Now.

Across the ocean in New York, students slept on cold concrete outside Columbia and NYU, tents rising like islands of defiance beneath the city's skyscrapers. Their banners flapped in the wind — "Books, Not Bombs," "End the Occupation." Some wore keffiyehs over their shoulders; others held candles; their faces lit in soft orange halos as they read out the names of the dead. Journalists filmed, police waited, and still they stayed — reading, chanting, refusing to look away.

In The Hague, judges in black robes listened as South Africa presented its case before the International Court of Justice: State of Israel v. Genocide Convention. The chamber was cold, silent except for translators' voices. The words — "collective punishment," "targeting of civilians," "the destruction of life itself" — echoed in languages that Layla didn't speak but understood completely. The Court ruled for "provisional measures," ordering protection for civilians. Yet as the headlines spread, Gaza's lights remained off.

A week later, the UN General Assembly voted — 153 nations for an immediate ceasefire, ten against.

On Layla's cracked phone screen, the roll call played like a litany of conscience. Some names she knew only from the labels on sacks of aid or expired medicine. Others she had never heard before. The camera panned across the hall of flags, the applause

145

distant, abstract — a sound too clean to belong to their world. "The world agrees," she whispered. "But the sky here hasn't changed."

In Washington, marches swelled along Pennsylvania Avenue. Jewish, Muslim, and Christian faith groups walked side by side, rabbis and imams and priests linking arms. Their signs read: "Ceasefire Now," "No More Children Buried Beneath Rubble." Some held photos of families in Gaza — faces Layla might have passed once in the market or seen reflected in the mirror of her own daughter.

That night, under the low hum of their single lamp, Layla, Omar, and Mariam huddled together on the couch, watching the world through the glow of her phone. The video lagged, freezing every few seconds, but the images still reached them — people marching in the rain, voices echoing through cities they had only read about.

Layla pressed a hand to her mouth, overcome. "Look," she whispered, her voice trembling. "They're shouting for us." Mariam leaned closer, her eyes reflecting the screen's blue light. "Maybe," she said softly, "the world finally remembered we exist."

Omar didn't answer at first. He watched the footage of strangers waving flags, chanting words that once felt impossible to say aloud — Palestine, freedom, life. Then he nodded slowly.

"Or maybe," he said, his voice rough, "they finally learned what love looks like."

Outside, the sea was calm. The sky buzzed faintly with distant drones. But for the first time in years, Gaza felt less alone — as if the walls themselves had heard marching feet far, far away.

After disputed allegations, UNRWA's funding was suspended by several donor states. Within weeks, the agency's warehouses stood silent — their metal doors padlocked, murals of blue UN logos fading beneath the dust. Families lined up before dawn outside the closed distribution canters, clutching ration cards that no longer promised anything. The lines still formed out of habit, as if waiting itself were a kind of prayer.

Rice and flour disappeared first, then lentils, then canned meat. Markets tried to fill the gap: stallholders sold single eggs wrapped in paper, cooking oil by the cup, sugar by the spoon. The price of bread doubled in two weeks. Mothers mixed ground animal feed with wheat to stretch their dough. Children carried home loaves that tasted of bitterness and survival.

Hospitals were no better. When the main power plant failed again, entire wards ran on car batteries and solar fragments scavenged from bombed rooftops. At Al-Shifa, doctors used the light from their phones to stitch wounds. In maternity units, nurses fanned newborns to keep them breathing through blackouts. The air smelled of iodine, sweat, and melted plastic from overworked wires.

And yet — life refused to surrender.

In narrow alleys, wedding songs still drifted from courtyards; a bride's white dress sewn from scraps of fabric shimmered like defiance. Children still flew kites made from rubbish bags. Fishermen still pushed their boats to the six-mile line, chasing both fish and freedom. Even laughter survived — hoarse, fragile, but real — echoing through the ruins like birds that refused to migrate.

In their small apartment on Al-Rimal Street, Layla rationed water by the jug, marked the hours of electricity on the wall, and counted every candle left in the drawer. She kept a pot of mint alive on the balcony, watering it with the last rinse from their dishes. The leaves were small but fragrant — the scent of persistence.

Mariam had turned words into resistance. Each evening, during the two hours of current, she typed on her aging laptop, the keys sticking from humidity. Her essays reached online forums and youth networks abroad — translated into Arabic, English, Spanish, and French.

"Our resilience," she wrote, "is not a slogan. It's what we do between airstrikes — repair, teach, sing, remember. We live not because the bombs stop, but because the heart refuses to." Layla printed the essay on the back of an old school notice and taped it to the fridge. "So, we don't forget our own voice," she said.

In August, Layla turned forty. The day passed quietly, the electricity out since morning. At dusk, Omar returned from the reconstruction site, his clothes still dusted with cement. In his hand, he carried a single olive branch, freshly cut from a tree near Beit Lahiya. Its leaves shimmered silver-green in the half-light.

"It's all I could find," he said, a shy smile breaking through the fatigue. Layla took it gently, brushing her thumb across the cool leaves. "It's all we ever needed," she answered. For a moment, the room felt full again — of warmth, of breath, of something unbreakable.

That night, by candlelight, she opened her old journal, its pages warped from humidity and time. The flame flickered against the blue paint of the walls as she wrote:

"They call us statistics.

But every number here has a heartbeat.

Every ruin has a story.

Every love, a future still insisting on itself."

When she set the pen down, the generator outside had already fallen silent. The world narrowed to the soft hiss of the candle and the slow pulse of the sea beyond the window.

A wind swept through the balcony, carrying the familiar scent of salt and diesel, of a shoreline both captive and eternal. Layla looked out, imagining the same waves touching the beaches of Cyprus, Alexandria, Jaffa — the shared rhythm of water that no wall could contain. For a heartbeat, she felt Gaza breathing with the rest of the world — unseen, unheard, but alive. And in that fragile stillness, survival itself became the truest form of love.

Vignette — A Letter in the Rubble

Weeks after the last airstrike, when the bulldozers finally reached Al-Rimal, aid workers clearing the ruins uncovered something small between the concrete and sand —

a notebook, its cover burned at the edges, held together by a strand of red thread.

The pages were singed and salt-stained, but a few lines survived, handwritten in careful Arabic:

"To whoever finds this —

We built our house out of laughter and borrowed wood.

We survived on lentils, stories, and hope.

Tell the world we loved, even when it hurt.

Tell them we were alive."

At the bottom, there was no name — only a faint sketch of three figures: a man, a woman, and a child beneath a tree whose roots disappeared into the page.

When a photograph of the notebook was shared online by an aid worker, it spread quickly — reposted, translated, and captioned across languages. The most common caption read: "Gaza writes its own love story."

And it did — not through headlines or reports, but through the fragments left behind.

Every letter, every mural, every rebuilt wall was part of a collective story written in dust and breath — proof that memory, even scorched, could still speak.

1.11 CHAPTER 10 – BENEATH THE DUST, THE ROOTS

"They tried to bury us.
They didn't know we were seeds."
— Old proverb, written on a Gaza wall.

Part 1 – The Quiet After

Morning comes slowly to Gaza — as if even the light hesitates before crossing the sky. The sea hums softly against the shore, its rhythm older than the city itself. Waves carry both salt and memory, touching the sand like a mother testing the forehead of a sleeping child.

From the rooftops, the muezzin's call mingles with the buzz of generators, the flutter of laundry in the wind, and the distant cries of gulls circling the harbour. The air smells of brine, metal, and warm bread rising from clay ovens below. It is a new day — but in Gaza, newness never comes empty. Every dawn carries what the night could not bury: the echoes of loss, the quiet defiance of survival.

Layla wakes before sunrise to the sound of Omar's footsteps in the courtyard. Through the half-open door, she sees him watering their garden — a mosaic of life grown from ruin. The plants cling to the cracked walls as if refusing to let go mint, thyme, and jasmine rooted in broken buckets, their green leaves trembling under drops of recycled water. Their scent mingles with dust and oil, a fragile perfume of persistence.

Under her breath, Layla whispers the prayer her mother taught her during shelling: "Let today be gentler than yesterday." The

151

words drift into the morning air, half prayer, half spell — and like everything in Gaza, they are both habit and hope.

Part 2 – Memory as Inheritance

Every Gazan family keeps a box of memories — their unofficial archive of identity, a museum of what the wars couldn't erase.

In Layla's home, it sits on a shelf above the kitchen table: an old metal biscuit tin, its lid rusted, its corners dented from years of being packed and unpacked during evacuations. Inside are the fragments of their life — pieces that mean more than any document ever could.

Omar's construction union badge, still dusted with cement from the days he helped rebuild the city after the 2014 war. Layla's teaching certificate, edges browned from candlelight when she studied during blackouts. A faded photo of their first home, the one flattened in that same summer — their smiles half-vanished beneath a crease.

Mariam's first drawing, a house with no walls and a single bright sun above it, titled in careful handwriting: Safe Place. And at the very bottom, wrapped in cloth, a small mosaic tile from Jaffa, salvaged from her grandmother's destroyed home — passed down like a sacred relic, smooth as a worn prayer stone.

"These," Omar says softly whenever they open it, "are our passports — proof that we existed before the borders did."

Sometimes, during long power cuts, they sit together by the glow of a single candle and open the tin. The room fills with silence — not emptiness, but reverence.

Layla lifts the tile and begins to tell the story her grandmother told her: how in 1948, during the Nakba, she fled Jaffa with a sack of flour, her wedding ring hidden in her shoe. She walked for days beneath burning skies, following the tide of the displaced until she reached a refugee camp that no longer exists — a place where tents became houses and grief became routine, and yet people planted fig trees beside canvas walls. "We built lives out of wind," her grandmother used to say.

Omar adds his own story — of his father, a fisherman who once sailed beyond the six-mile limit despite patrol warnings. They caught him, seized his boat, and left him stranded on the shore. But at dawn the next day, barefoot and unshaken, he borrowed a neighbour's skiff and went back to sea.

"He said the water doesn't belong to borders," Omar recalls. "It belongs to those who remember it."

Mariam listens, her pencil scratching softly as she sketches their stories — her grandmother's footsteps, her grandfather's boat, the biscuit tin itself, each line a thread in a larger tapestry. She doesn't draw for nostalgia. She draws to preserve — to make visible what cannot be carried through checkpoints or stored on clouds.

In Gaza, memory is not a luxury. It is a discipline, a testimony, a quiet act of resistance. It is the way they prove, to themselves and to the world, that even when buildings fall, the roots remain.

Part 3 – The Land Remembers

Late summer in Gaza does not fade easily. It clings — to the cracked rooftops, to the sand that still smells of smoke, to the faces of those who have learned that even the calm has weight.

Now, as August melts into September 2025, the air softens just enough to remind people that seasons still exist. The sun descends slower, kinder, the light staying longer on the rooftops before surrendering to dusk.

After months of bombardment and silence, the sky has begun to sound like itself again — seagulls, wind, prayer, waves.

Across Gaza City, colour returns where no one expected it. Anemones bloom in craters left by airstrikes, their red petals trembling like wounds that chose to stay open so the world would remember. Between broken concrete, wild poppies rise in stubborn rows. Ivy threads through the metal of a collapsed balcony, wrapping green fingers around bullet-marked stone. Even destruction, here, insists on rooting.

Omar spends his mornings with a group of volunteers known simply as The Rootkeepers. They are teachers, farmers, teenagers, and elders — men and women who once tended groves that no longer exist. They move together through streets still heavy with dust, carrying spades, saplings, and water in salvaged jugs. Their clothes are patched, their hands raw. Every olive tree they plant is more than a gesture — it is a declaration that something beneath the soil is still alive.

Each sapling bears a tag tied with wire or ribbon. Names written in blue ink: a teacher, a medic, a poet, a child. Some bear only initials — when an entire family was erased and no one remained to write them fully. Together, the trees form a new kind of forest, one that remembers more than it shades.

The elders say the olive tree is holy because it refuses to die. Even burned, it returns from its roots. Even cut, it bleeds silver sap and grows again.

In Beit Hanoun stands a living testament — a 600-year-old olive tree that survived every bombardment. Its trunk is hollow, its bark torn open like an old scar, yet each spring it turns green again.

People call it The Witness. When the wind moves through its branches, it sounds like a whispering crowd — voices layered through centuries, prayers that never found walls to echo from. Children play in its roots; elders leave cups of water beneath it, "so memory doesn't dry," they say with a half-smile that carries a thousand stories.

This year, the planting carries new meaning.

After the 18 August 2025 ceasefire — a 60-day truce brokered in Cairo and Doha between Israel and Hamas — the skies have remained mostly quiet, though everyone still listens for echoes. It is not peace, not yet, but a pause that feels like breath returning to lungs long starved of air. For the first time in months, the sea looks blue again instead of ash grey.

The ceasefire opened Gaza's crossings for limited humanitarian aid. China sent relief planes through Egypt, their silver bellies low over Rafah, releasing pallets of flour, tents, and solar lamps marked with red characters and small white doves. Italian and Spanish humanitarian ships followed soon after, arriving under UN coordination, their decks stacked with desalination units, medicine, and school tents painted with children's drawings from Naples and Seville.

For three days, the shoreline turned into a living miracle. People, stood on the dunes waving flags and scarves as aid boats off-loaded boxes into small local ferries. Men formed human chains to pass supplies hand to hand; women clapped; children ran beside the water shouting the names of distant cities they had only ever read about. For once, the horizon shimmered not with smoke, but with the hum of engines bringing life.

Layla's classroom filled with the murmur of students. The windows were covered with plastic that fluttered like slow-beating wings. Electricity came and went in brief flickers, but no one cared.

On the board, written in chalk, was a single line from Mahmoud Darwish: "We suffer from an incurable disease called hope."

They read his words by flashlight and candle, their voices uneven but determined. Outside, the wind pressed against the plastic sheets like a heartbeat. For a moment, the sound of children reading poetry drowned out the hum of drones far above.

Part 4 – A Generation Rises

Mariam is sixteen now — that uncertain age balanced between childhood and something harder. Her hair, once braided by her mother each morning, now escapes in loose strands as she hunches over a laptop salvaged from a destroyed school. On its back, she's drawn a small sun with a marker, the word "Tomorrow" written beneath it in English.

Each day after classes, she walks to a shipping container painted sky-blue, the letters "Tech for Life" stencilled across its side in fading black. Inside, the hum of solar panels powers a fragile miracle: rows of refurbished laptops glowing faintly even when the power grid outside collapses. The whir of their fans competes with the noise of generators and the distant roll of the sea.

"This," Mariam tells the younger kids who crowd around her, "is our window to the world." She grins as she adds, half-joking, "We'll build apps instead of walls." The children laugh, and she laughs too — but behind her smile sits a quiet determination, something she inherited from Layla's patience and Omar's endurance.

Their projects stretch from practical to poetic. One small team code an app to track rainfall for local farmers, helping them plan when to plant in fields scarred by tanks. Another group builds a chatbot that teaches English through Palestinian proverbs.

When it says, "Patience is the key to relief," in both Arabic and English, the students repeat the words aloud like a lesson and a prayer at once.

Mariam leads the project that moves her most: a digital archive of Gaza's lost landmarks — the schools, libraries, murals, and markets that once stood before the bombings. They rebuild them from drone photos, fragments of memories, and hand-drawn sketches from the community. Each upload preserves what once was — pixel by pixel, memory by memory.

"If the world won't rebuild our streets," Mariam tells her classmates, "Then we'll rebuild them in data." No one argues; they simply nod and keep typing.

Outside, the sounds of hammers and keyboards mingle — two kinds of rebuilding, two languages of survival. The city, she thinks, is learning to speak again, not through speeches or noise, but through creation.

At her age, children in other countries are learning to drive, taking swimming lessons, dreaming of concerts, college, and summer vacations.

Mariam dreams too — of stable electricity, of school weeks without funerals, of coding without counting battery percentage. She scrolls through the photos her friends abroad send crowded city streets, neon lights, a park filled with leaves untouched by smoke. "One day," she writes in reply, "you'll visit our coast when it's free again."

Some of her friends have already left — a scholarship to Canada, a remote coding course in Türkiye, a design internship in Malaysia. Their messages arrive between power cuts, glowing on her screen for seconds at a time, fragments of normalcy flickering in and out of Gaza's uneven light. Others have stayed: one studies medicine in Khan Younis, another helps rebuild classrooms in Beit Lahia. They stay connected through group chats filled with voice notes, sketches, poems, plans — the digital thread of a generation that refuses to be cut off.

"We don't have airports," one of them writes, "but we have Wi-Fi." In that single line, the absurdity and beauty of survival coexist.

Mariam updates her blog, Echoes of Tomorrow, each night by candlelight. Her words reach strangers she's never met — a teenager in Barcelona who sends her photos of the sea, a teacher in Seoul who shares her posts with students, a grandmother in Nairobi who writes, "Your hope keeps me awake."

Her latest entry reads: "Hope is not what we wait for. It's what we build — code by code, seed by seed — until it stands tall enough to shade us."

When she finishes typing, the power flickers out again. Outside, the solar lights along the Corniche blink to life, their soft glow spilling over the sand. The sea is quiet tonight, its waves gentle and even, as if the world has finally taken a breath.

From their rooftop, Layla watches her daughter's reflection in the dark window — her face lit only by the faint blue of the screen. Omar, sitting beside her, whispers, "She's growing roots where we planted only dust." And, somewhere beyond the city, in the quiet fields of Beit Hanoun, an olive sapling planted earlier that summer begins to bear its first fruit.

Part 5 – The Return of Festivals

For the first time in more than a decade, Gaza's Corniche glows with lights not from flares or drones, but from lanterns and laughter. Along the seafront promenade, tents bloom like bright sails in the wind — white, crimson, turquoise — each one sheltering something made by hand: embroidery from Rafah, clay pots from Beit Hanoun, honey jars from the orange groves of Deir al-Balah.

The air carries the mingled scents of cardamom, roasted corn, and sea salt, a fragrance of celebration and survival. Children chase kites painted with doves; vendors call out over the hum of generators repurposed to power string lights. A young boy balances on a crate, reciting verses by Mahmoud Darwish into a borrowed microphone. The crowd applauds, their hands glowing in the lamplight. "His words used to be whispered," an old man murmurs, "and now they fly."

Layla's students perform a short play they've written themselves — A City That Refused to Vanish. They wear costumes sewn from donated fabric, stitched by the women's cooperative. When they bow, the audience stands. Layla wipes her eyes, laughing through tears. "They remembered every line," she whispers to Omar.

Nearby, Omar's cooperative displays their latest creation — eco-bricks made from recycled plastic and sand, sturdy enough to rebuild benches along the Corniche. Children drum on the hollow blocks, turning them into instruments. Omar grins, pride softening the lines of his face.

At another tent, Mariam livestreams the festival through her blog Echoes of Tomorrow. Her phone shakes slightly as she films, capturing the swirl of colours, the rhythm of tambourines, the unfiltered beauty of ordinary joy. Within hours, her post travels far beyond Gaza's borders. Comments pour in from London, Jakarta, São Paulo: "We've never seen Gaza like this." "Thank you for showing us the light."

The evening deepens into gold, then indigo. When fireworks bloom above the Mediterranean — red, green, white — the sky mirrors the flag they've never stopped carrying in their hearts.

159

The sound cracks open the air, and for a heartbeat, some children flinch, their memories too fresh.

Layla draws Mariam close, her hand over her daughter's heart. "See?" she whispers. "Even joy can be rebuilt." Mariam looks toward the sea, where the reflections of the fireworks ripple like living constellations. For the first time, the horizon feels open — not as an edge, but as a beginning.

Part 6 – Closing Reflections: Beneath the Dust

At sunset, the family walks again toward the shore. The sea lies calm — a vast mirror of amber light where the day slowly exhales its last breath. Waves curl and sigh against the sand, carrying the scent of salt, diesel, and distant fires — the unmistakable perfume of Gaza at peace for a moment.

Around them, fishermen mend their nets with patient fingers, their silhouettes dark against the molten sky. Teenagers race along the Corniche on bicycles rebuilt from scraps, laughter trailing behind like banners in the wind. Lovers sit side by side on the sand, whispering prayers of gratitude, of endurance, of tomorrow.

Layla closes her eyes and breathes deeply. The air tastes of both salt and smoke, bitter and alive. "This place breaks," she says softly, "and we build. It burns, and we plant. We are not trapped — we are rooted."

Omar turns to her, his hands rough and scarred from years of rebuilding. The glow of sunset paints his face gold. "Roots grow deeper when the wind is strongest," he answers. "That's why we're still here."

Mariam crouches near the water's edge, tracing circles in the wet sand. The tide flows in and erases them gently, only for her to draw them again. She lifts a seashell, presses it to her ear, and listens. "It sounds like the city," she says — "the hum of generators, the calls to prayer, the laughter, the waves." Layla smiles. "Maybe it's the sea remembering us."

They sit together as the horizon fades — not into darkness, but into continuity. The light lingers like an unfinished promise. Tomorrow will bring its shortages, its waiting, its small triumphs. The world beyond the walls may still turn slowly, but here, something endures. Because beneath every ruin, every scar, every grain of dust — the roots remain. And in those roots live all the stories, all the voices, all the quiet defiance of a people who refused to vanish.

The sea whispers again, folding the city's heartbeat into its rhythm — steady, endless, unbroken.

Epilogue – For Gaza

For those who left, and those who stayed.

For the builders who raise walls from dust, for the dreamers who sketch cities on the margins of maps.

For the teachers who light minds under flickering bulbs, and the mothers who turn scarcity into supper and song.

For the children who learned the sound of drones before thunder — and still found the courage to laugh.

For the fishermen who sail before dawn, trusting the sea though it has betrayed them a hundred times.

For the students who write their essays on cracked screens, their words crossing borders their bodies cannot.

For every doctor who stitched wounds by phone light, every artist who painted beauty on broken walls, every voice that refused silence.

The world may see rubble. But we — we know the truth.

Gaza breathes.

It inhales the dust of yesterday and exhales the promise of tomorrow.

Every sunrise, it begins again — uninvited, unstoppable.

And every time the dust settles, something green rises through — a mint leaf, a jasmine vine, a child's voice whispering, "We're still here."

Because beneath the debris, beneath the blockade, beneath the endless waiting, there is always a pulse.

It beats in the soil, in the sea, in the hearts that refuse to forget.

This is not survival. It is existence — blooming.

#

1.12   CHAPTER 11 — PATHWAYS TO A DURABLE PEACE

"Peace is not a pause between wars — it's the work of the living."

Part 1 — The Aftermath That Never Ends

Gaza was a geography of both destruction and endurance. Satellite images released in June 2025 by UN OCHA confirmed that over 62 percent of housing units were damaged or destroyed after the late-2024 assault. Yet, in the aerial grey, there were also threads of green — narrow rooftop farms stitched across ruins, balcony gardens where tomatoes climbed over shrapnel-pocked railings.

Omar stood on one of those rooftops, adjusting a solar panel salvaged from a broken streetlight. He had rewired it with copper stripped from old phone cables. Below him, children played in what used to be a courtyard, their laughter rose like a challenge to gravity. "We build the future from pieces of yesterday," he murmured.

Layla was teaching again — not in a school of brick and tile, but under a UNICEF tent classroom erected beside the ruins of Al-Shati School. The tent walls flapped in the wind; the alphabet charts were drawn on flour-sack paper. "Education is reconstruction of the mind," she told her students, writing the words in chalk on the fabric wall. When the gusts rattled the poles, it sounded like applause.

That month, the World Health Organization warned that 92 percent of Gaza's residents had limited or no access to safe water. Desalination plants, running at one-third capacity for lack of fuel, produced barely half the daily minimum requirement. Cholera clusters appeared in northern camps; malnutrition among children under five reached 35 percent, the highest in a decade. Only 18 percent of hospitals were fully functional; the rest operated with intermittent electricity and stockpiles of expired antibiotics.

Omar's engineering cooperative had shifted from rebuilding homes to installing micro-solar grids in courtyards and mosques, part of a pilot project launched with UNDP and local technicians in July 2025. "If the state cannot power us," he said, "the sun will." Each panel lit a handful of bulbs and a single refrigerator — enough for one family's medicine, one night's dignity.

By August, new community kitchens funded by World Central Kitchen and local women's groups fed over 50,000 people daily across the Strip. Layla volunteered twice a week, stirring lentil soup in great iron pots, her sleeves rolled to the elbows. "We cook," she said, "because cooking means there's still a table somewhere waiting to be filled."

International attention had dimmed again — the news cycle had moved on — but reconstruction committees continued their work under tarp roofs. UNRWA's June–September bulletin listed eight hundred new temporary classrooms, forty-seven repaired wells, and twenty-three kilometres of water pipe laid by local hands.

In the evenings, Omar and Layla sat on the roof, their daughter Mariam beside them drawing suns with chalk on the concrete.

"Why do you always draw the sun?" Layla asked.

"Because it always comes back," Mariam replied.

Below, the muezzin's call mingled with the clatter of hammers — Gaza's new heartbeat. Amid disease, shortage, and fatigue, life persisted not as denial but as decision. Peace, Omar thought, would never arrive by decree; it was already here, pieced together each day by those who refused to stop living.

Part 2 — The Global Reckoning

Beyond Gaza, the world was changing — slowly, unevenly, but undeniably.

The horror of the 2023–2024 war had forced a moral confrontation that no government could fully escape. By mid-2025, the reverberations had spread from courtrooms to city squares, from chancelleries to classrooms.

At The Hague, the International Court of Justice (ICJ) continued its hearings in South Africa v. Israel, a case that had come to define the decade's conscience. In June 2025, the Court received its third round of compliance reports. UN observers confirmed that humanitarian access remained "severely constrained," despite pledges of reform. Expert witnesses — among them former UN relief chiefs and epidemiologists — presented data showing that famine conditions persisted in northern Gaza. The judges listened in silence, pens scratching like slow metronomes of history.

Across the courtyard, journalists huddled in the Dutch rain. One of them whispered, "This is what accountability sounds like — paperwork and patience."

The International Criminal Court (ICC) moved in parallel, its investigations broadening beyond the battlefield to include obstruction of aid and targeting of civilian infrastructure. In August 2025, ICC Prosecutor Karim Khan announced that the evidence-review phase was complete and that decisions on arrest warrants were imminent under consideration as of late

165

2025. It was a cautious sentence, but in Gaza it echoed like thunder.

At the United Nations, the diplomatic stalemate began to crack. In July 2025, the Security Council adopted Resolution 2743 — a measure calling for an independent international monitoring mission to oversee the reconstruction corridors through Rafah and Kerem Shalom. It passed with thirteen votes in favour; only the United States abstained. The resolution's passage was hailed as "the first coordinated step toward durable humanitarian access since 2007."

In Geneva, the World Health Assembly devoted an emergency session to Gaza's public-health collapse. Delegates watched video briefings from doctors performing surgery by flashlight, from children queueing for water. The session ended with a unanimous vote to fund a regional medical air-bridge linking Gaza's remaining hospitals to facilities in Cairo and Amman — a modest lifeline, but a real one.

Meanwhile, the streets spoke louder than the halls.

In London, on June 8, 2025, nearly 600 000 people marched from Hyde Park to Parliament Square — the largest demonstration since the Iraq War. Handmade banners fluttered under summer rain: "Ceasefire Means Ceasefire."

In Berlin, artists projected the names of Gazan children onto the façade of the Reichstag.

In New York, activists formed a human chain around the UN Headquarters, holding candles through the night as the East River reflected their light.

In Jakarta, Nairobi, Santiago, and Sydney, solidarity rallies crossed lines of religion and ideology.

Digital spaces mirrored the streets. The hashtag #CeasefireForHumanity replaced #StopTheSiege by late July 2025, trending across every major platform. Online campaigns raised millions for medical relief, while journalists and citizen archivists compiled open-source databases of destroyed schools and missing persons.

Governments, too, began to shift. Spain, Ireland, Slovenia, and Norway formally recognized the State of Palestine in May 2025, prompting wider discussions within the European Union. By September, France had announced that recognition was "no longer a question of if, but when." The African Union and Latin American Parliament issued joint communiqués demanding a "permanent lifting of the blockade and an international peace framework within the year."

The geopolitical calculus was changing — less from sudden conscience than from sustained fatigue. As one diplomat at Turtle Bay confessed to a reporter, "The world has learned that Gaza is not only a tragedy — it's a mirror."

By autumn 2025, that mirror reflected something new: a planet reconsidering its tolerances. From the courthouses of Europe to the marches of Johannesburg, from policy rooms in Doha to student campuses in Montreal, the demand was no longer abstract. It had become a sentence shared across languages and continents: "Justice is not revenge. It's repair." And in that fragile reckoning — legal, moral, and human — the first outlines of a different future began to appear.

Part 3 — Diplomacy and Deadlock

By mid-2025, diplomacy had become both a performance and a prayer. The world's cameras turned again toward Cairo, where delegations from the United States, Qatar, and Egypt convened in a marble hall that had seen more failed peace talks than weddings. The air was thick with protocol and cigarette smoke. Each side arrived carrying both documents and ghosts.

The agenda, thin as parchment, rested on three fragile pillars:

Hostage and prisoner exchanges,

Humanitarian corridors,

A phased reconstruction plan under international supervision.

Behind closed doors, translators whispered, pens tapped, tempers simmered. Every breakthrough was followed by a pause — not of relief, but of disbelief. Words like "security parameters" and "sequenced de-escalation" filled the communiqués, while outside the conference hall, the world counted bodies and aid trucks.

At one point, talks stalled for ten days over the definition of a "security zone" — a few kilometres of contested sand that became the hinge on which thousands of lives turned. Cairo's late-summer heat pressed against the windows; diplomats emerged from night-long sessions with eyes rimmed red.

Still, aid began to move — haltingly, conditionally, but undeniably. The Kerem Shalom crossing reopened for short windows in July and August, allowing convoys of flour, fuel, and medical supplies escorted by UN monitors. Each passage was preceded by hours of inspection and negotiation; sometimes the trucks idled for days under the desert sun.

The Rafah crossing, once Gaza's southern lung, remained tightly controlled. Egyptian security officials cited ongoing "reconstruction coordination" while hundreds of patients waited in tents on the border, medical referrals in hand. The waiting became its own ritual — names read aloud each morning, buses that sometimes never moved.

In Doha, envoys from Qatar and Norway, joined by the European Union, announced the Gaza Reconstruction Trust Fund, pledging $5 billion over five years. The fund, they promised, would prioritize housing, desalination, and renewable energy projects, with direct oversight by the UN Office for Project Services (UNOPS). But the fine print revealed a familiar fragility: disbursement depended on "sustained calm" and "verifiable security guarantees." In Gaza, those phrases translated to wait longer.

Omar followed the negotiations on a small radio powered by a hand-crank, the signal fading in and out between updates. He sat on the roof at dusk, the sky fading to rust over the ruins. "They talk about rebuilding roads," he said quietly. "But what about hearts?" Layla looked up from her lesson plans — papers weighted by stones to keep them from blowing away in the sea wind. "That's our work," she replied. "They can only build what we still believe in."

In September 2025, a draft of the "Cairo Framework for Peace and Reconstruction" was circulated among the delegations. It outlined a twelve-month ceasefire, monitored by an international observer force composed of UN, Egyptian, and Jordanian contingents — unarmed, humanitarian, symbolic. The plan envisioned a demilitarized corridor for aid, the return of detainees, and a joint committee to oversee rebuilding priorities.

But politics remained the quiet saboteur. Israeli coalition leaders, fractured over security concessions, hesitated to sign. Palestinian factions argued over representation. The Americans pushed for "sequenced trust-building," while the Qataris insisted on immediate humanitarian guarantees. Every side wanted peace — but on their own terms.

Meanwhile, on the ground, Gaza's patience had its own calendar. Children began school again under plastic roofs; water trucks rolled down cratered streets; fishermen returned to the six-mile zone under watchful patrols. Each ordinary act was a kind of diplomacy too — negotiation not of treaties, but of survival.

One evening, as Omar turned the radio dial, static blurred the voice of a BBC correspondent reporting from Cairo: "Sources close to the talks say progress is slow, but hope remains." He smiled bitterly. "Hope always remains," he said. "It's what they leave us when everything else is taken." Layla placed her hand on his, her fingers streaked with chalk and dust. "Then we'll build with that," she said. "Brick by brick. Word by word."

Beyond their rooftop, the lights of Gaza flickered — a mosaic of resilience stitched across darkness. In the hum of distant generators and the whisper of the sea, the city waited, as it always had, between diplomacy and deadlock.

Part 4 — The Small Bridges

Beyond the conference tables, in Gaza's narrow streets and makeshift classrooms, quieter forms of peace were already being practiced. Even amid siege, quiet forms of dialogue began to surface — not in parliaments or plenaries, but in hospital corridors, classrooms, and across unstable internet connections. They were the kind of bridges built not with steel, but with patience.

In Haifa, a group of Israeli and Palestinian doctors launched a telemedicine initiative in early August 2025, funded jointly by Physicians for Human Rights–Israel and Médecins du Monde. Using a low-bandwidth platform developed by medical students at the Technion, they began holding remote consultations for Gaza's overburdened clinics.

The connections were fragile — sometimes lasting ten minutes before power cut off — but in those minutes, lives were saved. Through the screen, Israeli cardiologist Dr. Yael Shani guided Rasha, a nurse at Al-Awda Hospital in northern Gaza, through an improvised cardiac procedure. When it succeeded, applause broke out on both sides of the call. "Medicine knows no borders," Dr. Shani said during a UN press briefing weeks later. "We speak one language — the pulse."

Elsewhere, teachers found their own ways to speak across walls. Layla began exchanging messages with Noa, a literature teacher from Tel Aviv, who had started a bilingual student correspondence project called Letters Across the Sea. The initiative began quietly, with support from UNESCO's Education for Peace program, and by September 2025, it had connected over four hundred students from Gaza, Jaffa, and Haifa.

Layla's tented classroom buzzed with excitement when the first envelope arrived — printed emails carried by a UN courier. The letters were simple: drawings of cats, stories about music, favourite foods, and questions about the sea.

Mariam wrote: "I don't want revenge. I want graduation without fear." Noa's student, Eitan, replied from a classroom overlooking the Mediterranean: "I want my friends to live without guilt."

The children began comparing skies — how in Gaza, stars looked brighter because of the blackouts, and how in Tel Aviv, light drowned them out. They wrote poems to the moon, who belonged to both. None of it made headlines. There were no press releases, no official statements. But in the quiet exchange of paper and ink, something irreversible was happening — empathy rediscovering its voice.

By October 2025, the project had expanded into virtual poetry circles, where teachers read Darwish, Leah Goldberg, and Yehuda Amichai side by side. Translators volunteered from both communities, and for a few minutes each week, screens became windows instead of walls.

One evening, as Layla read aloud a translated verse — "We travel like other people, but we return nowhere" — her students fell silent. Then Mariam whispered, "Maybe one day, we'll visit." Layla smiled. "Maybe one day, we won't have to visit — we'll just live."

Outside, the sky was clear. The sea murmured beyond the curfew line. Somewhere between Haifa and Gaza, signals flickered through cables buried in sand and saltwater — fragile bridges carrying the smallest, and therefore the strongest, kind of peace.

Part 5 — Rebuilding the Invisible

By September 2025, rebuilding no longer meant waiting for convoys or committees — it meant invention. The UN Development Programme (UNDP) had just launched the "Gaza Green Recovery Initiative," a project teaching youth how to reclaim their own future through solar engineering and eco-construction.

In a half-repaired workshop on the edge of Deir al-Balah, the hum of generators mixed with laughter. Omar stood at a worktable, his hands dusty with sand and melted plastic, showing a group of teenagers how to form eco-bricks from the remains of war — sand sifted from rubble, ash from burned homes, fragments of bottles. "Every block we press," he said, "is a small refusal to disappear."

He and Mariam took that lesson home. Together they built a greenhouse on the rooftop, framed from salvaged rebar and clear sheeting that once covered aid tents. Mint, tomatoes, and basil took root in buckets of reclaimed soil. Their scent drifted down the stairwell, carrying something miraculous: the smell of living things. Neighbours would pause in the doorway, breathing deeply as if inhaling memory itself.

Beyond their rooftop, the world pressed in.

On 4 September 2025, UN human-rights experts warned that journalists in Gaza were being silenced, urging states to act before truth itself vanished from the enclave. Then, on 16 September, the UN Commission of Inquiry on the Gaza Conflict released its final findings, concluding that Israel had committed acts of genocide. The report reached Gaza over crackling radios and broken internet, its words heavy yet vindicating — proof that the world had finally spoken aloud what Gazans had lived in silence.

At the end of September, the annual UN General Assembly in New York became consumed by Gaza's shadow. Diplomats repeated the words "ceasefire," "accountability," "reconstruction," yet even sympathetic envoys admitted that action lagged outrage. On 26 September, Israeli Prime Minister Benjamin Netanyahu stood before the same assembly and declared that Israel must "finish the job" against Hamas and free the remaining hostages. For those listening in Gaza, the phrase landed like an aftershock — a reminder that their peace was still a question mark.

Then, in early October, tragedy returned close to home: an aid distribution site run by UNRWA in Zeitoun was struck twice, killing workers and halting food delivery for thousands. The smell of dust and diesel filled the air again. Yet even then, life refused retreat.

Layla channelled her anger into purpose. With a small UNESCO grant, she launched "Peace Begins at Home," a community course in non-violent communication and civic storytelling. Classes met in a borrowed room behind a bakery, lit by candles during outages. Her students — mothers, young men, elders — took turns speaking of grief, dignity, and the daily art of patience. "We rebuild by speaking again," she told them. "If we lose words, we lose the map back to one another."

That same month, hope left its trace on concrete. Near the port, a group of young painters from Art for Tomorrow Gaza used leftover cement dust mixed with seawater to create a mural on a surviving warehouse wall. Two hands cupped a small seedling rising through rubble. Beneath it, in Arabic and English, they painted: "From the ashes, we grow."

The image spread faster than aid ever could. Shared first by a Haifa journalist, then echoed through timelines in Johannesburg, Santiago, and Dublin, it became the emblem of Gaza's second reconstruction — not of buildings, but of spirit.

Each evening, Omar walked Mariam past the mural. The air was warm and salt-scented, the paint still wet in places. "It's beautiful," she said, tracing the seedling with her eyes. He nodded. "Because it's still reaching upward."

In a world of reports and resolutions, that gesture — a child's fingertip following a painted leaf — was its own kind of truth: proof that even in the ruins of September and October, Gaza's people were still rebuilding the invisible — faith, language, and the stubborn rhythm of life itself.

Part 6 — The Global Mirror

While Gaza rebuilt from its ruins, the world outside began to face its own reflection. Each report, each protest, each policy debate echoed what the Strip had already learned — that destruction anywhere reveals fractures everywhere.

In Paris, students occupied the Sorbonne through early October 2025, demanding that France suspend arms exports to Israel and all conflict zones until international-law compliance could be verified. Their banners read "No Degrees on the Bones of Gaza." Similar occupations spread to Madrid, Brussels, and Montreal.

In Washington, D.C., congressional hearings reopened on the legality of U.S. military aid to Israel after the UN Commission of Inquiry's 16 September 2025 report, which concluded that Israel had committed acts of genocide in Gaza. Lawmakers argued over whether continued arms transfers could implicate the United States under Article III of the Genocide Convention. The debate reached the evening news but not yet the voting floor.

In Berlin, thousands of Jewish activists marched from Alexander Platz to the Brandenburg Gate, carrying candles and a banner stretched across the crowd: "Never Again Means Everyone."

It became one of the largest Jewish-led demonstrations in Germany since 1968, joined by Holocaust descendants who said they marched "to keep memory from becoming complicity."

The International Federation of Journalists issued its annual report that same month, confirming that 2023–2024 had been the deadliest period ever recorded for journalists, with Gaza at its epicentre — more than one hundred media workers killed, most inside their own homes or offices. UN human-rights experts, echoing their 4 September 2025 warning, urged governments to protect press freedom in conflict zones, declaring that "truth has become a frontline casualty."

Meanwhile, the planet itself convulsed. Earthquakes shook cities from Turkey to Japan, splitting highways and burying entire neighbourhoods in seconds. Wildfires turned the skies of

California, Greece, and Canada the colour of rust, while floods swallowed villages in Pakistan, Brazil, and Libya — waters rising so fast that entire families vanished overnight. Heat waves smothered Europe and the Middle East; rivers dried, crops withered, and millions fled homes that had become too hot to inhabit. The line between natural and political disaster blurred until it was no longer clear where negligence ended and nature began. Economists spoke of "the climate of inequality," and commentators began to call Gaza "the mirror of our century" — the place where technology, war, and morality collided in full view.

By 2022, Russia's invasion of Ukraine dragged Europe back into the vocabulary of siege — trenches, blackouts, air raids, refugees. Cities like Mariupol and Kharkiv became new synonyms for destruction, echoing Gaza's own wounds. A fragile cease-fire in 2025 brought only fleeting quiet before missiles fell again. Drone footage of burning apartment blocks flickered across the same screens that once showed Aleppo and Gaza, blurring continents into one shared catastrophe.

Elsewhere, unrest rippled outward. Sudan bled through another civil war; Yemen's hunger deepened; earthquakes rattled Afghanistan and Morocco; and fires devoured forests across the Amazon and Australia. By the summer of 2025, the planet seemed feverish — storms battering coastlines, drought gripping plains, and heat domes melting cities from Rome to Riyadh. Economists warned of permanent crisis, while journalists called it the age of overlap — where war, weather, and want merged into one unending emergency.

From her small room, Layla watched it all unfold on a cracked phone screen powered by Omar's solar battery. The scrolling felt endless — protests, speeches, data, grief — a world caught in its own algorithm of sorrow. Sometimes she lingered on images from Ukraine: a woman kneeling beside the ruins of her home, a child holding a candle in the snow. The devastation felt both distant and familiar — another reflection of Gaza's long night.

She turned the phone toward her daughter and whispered, "Maybe that's how peace begins — when the world finally sees itself in our ruins."

Part 7 — Lessons of History

While the world argued about accountability, Gaza listened — turning back to its own lessons of endurance. By mid-October 2025, Gaza had entered another kind of silence — not the quiet of peace, but the pause between heartbreaks. The world had grown used to speaking about the Strip in numbers: casualties, tons of rubble, aid trucks, megawatts. Yet inside Gaza, memory spoke in stories — and stories had their own arithmetic.

That month, at Birzeit University, a live-streamed lecture titled "A Century of Struggle" drew tens of thousands of listeners from Ramallah, Amman, Beirut, and even from Gaza's improvised classrooms where the internet signal blinked like a heartbeat. The historian stood before a cracked wall lined with old maps. He began with 1948, when more than 700 000 Palestinians were expelled or fled their homes during the Nakba, the catastrophe that scattered a people across borders and generations. He mentioned 1967, when occupation intensified; 1987 and 2000, marked by uprisings; and 1993, when the Oslo Accords brought administration rather than peace.

Then he reached the present. "The latest war," he said, "was born of everything unresolved." He traced the spark: the Hamas assault of 7 October 2023, in which roughly 1200 Israelis were killed and over 240 taken hostage, shocking even those long accustomed to violence. The response came in torrents — weeks of airstrikes, a ground invasion, and an unfolding siege that UN officials would later call "a collapse of civilization in slow motion."

By 2025, Gaza was described by aid agencies as unliveable:

– Over 38000 Palestinians killed, most of them women and children.

– Hospitals operating at less than one-fifth capacity.

– Water supplies reduced to less than two litres per person per day.

– Families displaced multiple times within a space no larger than a city.

"They refuse to surrender," the historian continued, "because surrender would mean vanishing — the final erasure of a people's claim to place." "Israel refuses to stop," he added softly, "because fear, after so many wars, has become the only thing that feels like control." He looked into the camera. "And peace does not come," he said, "because no one trusts the memory of the other." The hall was still. Even the livestream chat, usually frantic, paused. Then he concluded: "History doesn't end with war. It ends when memory stops teaching."

That night, under the dim pulse of a solar lamp, Layla typed those words into her next blog post. The lamp hummed faintly — powered by the same rooftop panels Omar had wired by hand.

She wrote about her grandmother's olive tree in Jaffa, planted before exile, its saplings now growing in Rafah sand. She wrote about the children in her tent-classroom, tracing the words peace, return, tomorrow onto torn notebook paper, their candles trembling in the wind. She wrote of the quiet act of teaching while the world debated genocide in courtrooms far away. "We don't surrender," she wrote, "because we are still being written."

Her post travelled far beyond the Strip. Within a day, it was shared across continents — translated into French, Spanish, and Japanese, quoted by human-rights organizations and student movements that had filled the streets of Paris, Berlin, and Cape Town throughout September and October. A journalist in South Africa called it "a dispatch from the edge of endurance — the voice that refuses to fade."

Outside, the October air carried the scent of mint and basil from their rooftop greenhouse. From the radio came the evening news — more UN debates, another ceasefire proposal delayed, another speech from New York promising accountability but naming no timeline. The words faded into static, replaced by the distant crash of waves.

Layla turned off the radio and listened to the night. "History is patient," she whispered. "Peace is still learning the lesson." Above her, the solar light glowed like a small star — fragile, persistent, and human. And beneath it, in that narrow apartment filled with the hum of life rebuilt from ruins, history continued to breathe — not as a record of endings, but as a promise still being written.

Part 8 — Toward a Possible Tomorrow

By autumn 2025, Gaza began to breathe again — not freely, but differently. The air carried a faint sense of direction. Beneath the ruin and rhetoric, something resembling possibility stirred.

In Cairo, diplomats convened under the marble dome of the Arab League headquarters to discuss what came to be called the "Cairo Framework." The proposal, first circulated in September 2025, called for: a five-year ceasefire guaranteed by regional and UN monitors, gradual lifting of the blockade under

179

international supervision, joint Israeli Palestinian environmental and energy projects, and an International Reconstruction Authority to manage recovery funds transparently.

The framework was endorsed by Egypt, Jordan, and the European Union, while the United States expressed "conditional support." Qatar and Norway pledged to co-chair the new Reconstruction Authority, promising oversight that would keep politics from strangling aid.

For the first time in years, the UN-monitored corridor through Kerem Shalom reopened for limited trade. Small cargoes of medical equipment, solar batteries, and seed stock passed through in mid-October. Satellite images released by UNOSAT showed cranes moving again in Gaza's southern industrial zones — fragile lines of motion against grey static.

Layla's women's cooperative, newly registered through the UNDP Green Recovery Initiative, prepared its first export: embroidered dresses sewn from recycled fabric, each tagged "Made in Gaza — Sewn in Hope." When the first modest payment arrived through a joint account in Cairo, she divided it without hesitation — half to the women who stitched, half to the community school that still taught under tarpaulin.

"Peace starts with payroll," Omar teased, smiling over the invoice.

"No," Layla replied, handing him a receipt. "Peace starts with trust."

Across the Strip, other small beginnings took root. The World Food Programme reported that over 2.1 million Gazans were receiving food aid regularly again, and 18 000 homes had been reconstructed since the ceasefire proposal's announcement. UNICEF reopened its child-learning centres; UNESCO funded new digital classrooms where displaced students logged into virtual lessons broadcast from Amman and Birzeit.

That same month, the UN Commission of Inquiry's September findings — confirming acts of genocide — continued to echo in world capitals. The International Criminal Court completed its evidentiary review and signalled that formal arrest warrants were imminent for crimes committed by all sides. Meanwhile, in New York, delegates spoke of Gaza as "the century's moral compass." Even sceptics admitted that the enclave had changed the conversation.

Omar stood beside Layla, their fingers intertwined. "Do you think peace will come in our lifetime?" he asked quietly. She watched a red-tipped kite vanish into the darkness. "Peace isn't coming," she said. "We're already walking toward it."

Weeks later, the UN issued its final 2025 assessment, titled "Gaza: Recovery and the Human Will." The report listed grim arithmetic but quiet progress: 2.1 million people receiving food assistance, 18 000 homes rebuilt or repaired, tens of thousands of students back in classrooms, 40 percent rise in female workforce participation, dozens of cross-border civic projects active, from journalism networks to seed-exchange initiatives.

Yet it ended not with data, but with a quote from a local teacher — Layla Hassan of Gaza City: "We no longer wait for peace to be given. We build it every morning when we open our eyes."

Omar read the report aloud that night, his voice trembling just slightly. Mariam sat nearby, sketching the new mural she'd seen by the port — two hands cupping a seedling, now brightened by salt and moonlight. It was not yet peace. But it was possible. And in Gaza, that word — possible — had become the most radical of all.

1.13 Chapter 12 Bearing Witness, and What You Can Do

"The opposite of war is not peace — it's memory."

Part 1 — The Work of Witness

Gaza, 2025.

The sea hums against the shore, indifferent to politics. From the rooftops, the water looks infinite — a line of blue that promises escape and denies it at once. The air carries the smell of dust, salt, and bread baked in community ovens. It is the same smell that has lingered through blockade and bombardment, through ceasefires and funerals — the smell of persistence.

It has been seventeen years since the blockade began, sealing Gaza's borders and turning a strip of coastline into the densest open-air prison in the world. The walls may have shifted, but the logic of control has not. Electricity still arrives in four-hour intervals; water still runs brackish from cracked pipes; drones still hum in the sky like mechanical bees. Yet life, stubbornly, insists on itself.

Layla sits on the balcony of the small apartment that survived the 2024 war — its walls pocked with shrapnel but still standing. Her daughter Mariam sketches beside her, drawing the sea with crayons donated by UNICEF. Omar is on the roof, adjusting the angle of a solar panel so it can catch the winter sun. He whistles softly — an old tune his father used to sing during curfews in the Second Intifada. In their quiet rhythm, there is something sacred: the choreography of survival that generations in Gaza have perfected.

Layla opens her laptop. The battery is half-full; she knows she has forty minutes before the next blackout. She types the final post for her blog, Echoes of Tomorrow. Her fingers hesitate on the keys before writing: "The world watched us break, then build again. If we have one gift, it's this: we know how to begin." She rereads the line and adds a final sentence: "Remember us not for how we died, but for how we lived."

Outside, the muezzin's call rolls across the city — soft, fractured by distance, echoing from minarets rebuilt over rubble. The sea answers with its own whisper. In the far distance, cranes rise like skeletal trees over new foundations — projects funded by Qatar and the UN Development Programme. Gaza rebuilds not once, but endlessly. It is both miracle and curse.

To bear witness, Layla has learned, is an act of rebellion. The world prefers silence; numbers are easier than names. Statistics flatten pain into policy. But storytelling — the kind that remembers faces, voices, gestures — resists erasure. That is why she writes: to defy oblivion.

Her blog began in the dark days of October 2023, when communications were cut and journalists were killed faster than headlines could be written. She typed by candlelight, sending her words through VPNs and unstable signals. Sometimes posts vanished before they uploaded. Other times, they travelled the world in seconds — shared by strangers who didn't know her but recognized truth when they read it.

"Every story that leaves Gaza is an escape tunnel," she once wrote. "Every word we send out is a breath we might not get back."

During the 2024 assault, documentation became survival. Citizens turned into chroniclers, filming destruction with dying phones, writing coordinates on scraps of paper for journalists abroad. The world saw, often for the first time, the unbearable intimacy of war: a father carrying his child through smoke, a nurse performing CPR in a hallway of dust, a teacher clutching exam papers under debris.

Among them was Motaz Azaiza, a young Palestinian photographer whose haunting images of Rafah and Khan Younis travelled across continents. His evacuation by the UN in early 2024 became a symbol of Gaza's collapsing freedom of speech — and its resilience. Another was Plestia Alaqad, a 22-year-old journalist who streamed live under bombardment, her trembling voice cutting through misinformation. According to Layla, these witnesses utilised their cameras as protective tools.

Witnessing is not only external. It is inward — remembering what dignity looks like even when dignity is rationed. In the shelters of 2024, Layla saw women boiling water on tin cans to sterilize milk bottles, children drawing suns over bomb craters, doctors using mobile phone lights to perform surgery. Each act, she realized, was a declaration: We exist.

Her friend Rasha, the nurse, once told her, "Hope isn't a feeling here. It's a muscle. If you don't use it, it dies." Rasha still works twelve-hour shifts in the maternity ward, helping mothers deliver under siege. When the power fails, she hand-pumps oxygen for the newborns, whispering prayers in the dark.

Now, in 2025, the world speaks the language of ceasefire again. Diplomats shake hands in Cairo and Geneva. Pledges are made, funds announced, conferences televised. Yet for those inside Gaza, peace is a verb — something done, not declared.

Omar's team of local masons rebuilds homes in Khan Younis using eco-bricks made from compressed sand and recycled plastic. They call the project "Roots," because everything they build grows from what was destroyed. Layla's women's cooperative has reopened, exporting embroidered dresses stitched from flour sacks — tatreez patterns carrying centuries of memory. Mariam helps manage the orders, learning to translate invoices from English to Arabic. Every package shipped abroad feels like a small message: We are still here.

In the evenings, the family gathers on the roof. The generator hums under an orange Mediterranean sky. Layla reads aloud from her journal: "The story of Gaza is not one of victimhood but of witness. To bear witness is to face reality directly, without ignoring hope or despair.

It means learning names, not just numbers. Stories, not just statistics."

Omar listens quietly, nodding. "And if no one listens?" he asks. Layla closes the book and looks toward the horizon. "Then we keep writing," she says. "Silence is what they want. Memory is what they fear."

Mariam releases her kite into the sea breeze. It rises slowly, fragile but free. On its tail, in bold letters, she has written: We live.

For a moment, the kite catches the last light of sunset — and in that instant, all the brokenness of Gaza feels like proof of something unbreakable.

Part 2 — What the World Saw

By 2025, a slow transformation was visible. The skyline, though scarred, shimmered with renewal. Rooftops sprouted gardens; solar panels lined balconies; community wells replaced broken pipes. In northern Gaza, engineers trained by local universities developed low-cost water filters built from crushed limestone and charcoal. Small victories, invisible to headlines, stitched life back together one thread at a time.

If Gaza's men rebuilt walls, its women rebuilt life itself. When cement was scarce, women mixed sand and crushed shells to make mortar strong enough for stoves and steps. When money ran out, they traded bread for labour, and kindness for survival. The heartbeat of the city came not from machines, but from kitchens, courtyards, and classrooms led by women whose strength rarely made the news.

Reconstruction, though noble, was never pure. Corruption seeped through like water through cracked stone. Every permit, every truck of gravel, every shipment of cement required signatures — and signatures required favours. Those with connections rebuilt faster; those without waited years. Bureaucracy became another form of siege.

Even after the bombardments of 2021 and 2023, Gaza's rebuilding moved slower than hope. Donors in Cairo had pledged $5.4 billion — only half ever arrived. Neighbourhoods like Shuja'iyya and Beit Hanoun remained ghostly skeletons of concrete and rebar, their silence heavier than the ruins themselves. By 2024, the UN reported that less than 35 percent of destroyed homes had been fully rebuilt; the rest were trapped in the maze of paperwork, checkpoints, and rival ministries. Reconstruction was never just about cement — it was about control.

Omar saw this every day at his construction cooperative.

"We wait months for approval to unload materials," he told Layla. "Meanwhile, someone with the right surname gets a permit in a week."

He spoke of contractors demanding extra fees to move supplies faster, of officials asking for donations in exchange for signatures.

One afternoon, a young man named Mahmoud showed Omar a folder swollen with papers.

"Seven years," he said bitterly. "Seven years of applications, stamps, and promises. My house still looks like a grave."

Some families paid smugglers to bring cement through tunnels before they were sealed — paying double the market price. Others bartered gold, furniture, even wedding rings for bags of gravel.

"We rebuild," one woman said, "but every wall costs a piece of dignity."

Layla joined a women's advocacy group calling for transparency in reconstruction projects. They met weekly in a community hall lit by candles when the power failed. They kept ledgers, documented complaints, interviewed families, and published reports in local papers and online platforms like We Are Gaza Voices.

"We are not only victims," Layla told them. "We are witnesses."

Their small movement drew attention — and discomfort. An anonymous note slipped under the door warned them to stop asking questions. But Layla refused.

"If we stay silent," she said, "we become part of the corruption too."

By late 2024, the group had partnered with local journalists and UN Women to monitor reconstruction funds. Together, they exposed the diversion of aid materials — tons of cement sold illegally on the black market, medical supplies resold in private clinics. Their findings sparked brief but fierce public debate.

Change was slow, uneven, and sometimes punished — but awareness had begun. For the first time, families demanded receipts instead of promises. Community committees formed to track deliveries, engineers volunteered to verify projects. Omar told Layla one night,

"Maybe we can't fix the system. But if we shine a light on it, at least they'll have to build in daylight."

Rebuilding Gaza was never only about concrete. It was about rebuilding trust. And in that fragile space between survival and accountability, people like Layla and Mahmoud learned a hard truth: that even under blockade, integrity itself could become an act of defiance.

Across the Strip, small miracles began to take shape — sewing cooperatives in half-collapsed rooms, micro-bakeries in alleyways, literacy classes beneath tarpaulin tents. UN Women reported that by late 2024, over 23 percent of Gaza's small businesses were run by women, many from homes rebuilt with aid loans or community funds. These women were not just earning an income — they were reweaving the social fabric war had torn apart.

Fatima, once simply Layla's neighbour, became known as the Soup Lady. Each evening, she cooked for a dozen families using whatever she could find — lentils, rice, sometimes only herbs and salt. Her courtyard smelled of cumin and smoke, her laughter louder than the shelling had ever been.

"If we feed each other," she said, stirring the pot, "we will not forget who we are."

Layla often helped after teaching at the women's centre. Together they kept a register of families most in need — widows, displaced mothers, orphans. What began as a cooking rota grew into a network of solidarity. Farmers donated vegetables; fishermen left small bags of dried sardines at doorsteps. In a place where 70 percent of households faced food insecurity, sharing became its own economy.

At the community centre in Deir al-Balah, Layla taught computer literacy three days a week. Her students — nurses, artists, young mothers — learned to type and design under the glow of phone screens and generator hums.

"When the world closes a door," Layla told them, "Open a window online."

Through unstable internet connections, they joined global workshops and sold handmade crafts abroad. One student, Rawan, designed embroidered laptop sleeves; another built a digital art gallery to share women's stories. Technology was no luxury — it was liberation.

Layla partnered with NGOs like Women for Change and CARE International to expand the program. With microgrants as small as $200, they bought used sewing machines and second-hand smartphones.

By mid-2025, their online marketplace, made in Gaza — Stitched in Hope, had shipped more than four hundred items to Europe and the Gulf. Each dress and scarf carried a handwritten tag: "From our hands to your heart."

"These women are the quiet architects of recovery," said an Oxfam field officer visiting the centre. "While politics stalls, they rebuild the soul of Gaza."

Beyond livelihoods, they built community. When schools stayed closed after bombings, Layla and others transformed classrooms into day centres. They played, taught, and listened. Together with UNICEF volunteers, they ran art workshops where children painted what words could not express. One boy drew his mother holding a house made of light.

At night, when the city dimmed under another blackout, Layla walked home past balconies flickering with candlelight. On each one, women mended clothes, rocked babies, studied by the blue glow of phones. None of them called themselves heroes — yet everything they did was heroic.

By 2025, the Palestinian Central Bureau of Statistics reported that women's labour-force participation in Gaza had doubled since 2019 — from 11 to 22 percent. The number seemed small, but behind it were thousands of stories: of Layla, of Fatima, of every mother who refused to surrender her child's tomorrow.

"They said we were weak," Fatima laughed once, wiping flour from her hands. "But the world forgets who kneads the bread and holds the house together."

When the spring festival returned to Gaza's Corniche, Layla's network catered for half the city. They decorated stalls with tatreez embroidery, baked ma'amoul dusted with sugar, and sang old harvest songs. Foreign visitors photographed them as symbols of resilience, but to Layla they were more than symbols. They were the spine of Gaza — bending but unbroken, quiet but unyielding.

These women carried Gaza on their shoulders — balancing grief, work, and hope. They built without blueprints, healed without recognition, and dreamed without rest.

They did not wait for peace to be declared.

They created it — one loaf, one lesson, one heartbeat at a time.

The year 2024 marked one of the deadliest conflicts in Gaza's history. According to the United Nations Office for the Coordination of Humanitarian Affairs (OCHA), by the end of that year: Over 37,000 Palestinians were killed, two-thirds of them women and children.

More than 75,000 injured.

1.9 million displaced — 85% of the population.

Over 60% of housing units destroyed or damaged.

Schools, hospitals, and mosques hit repeatedly despite protected status.

In January 2025, the International Court of Justice found it "plausible" that Israel's actions in Gaza could constitute genocide and ordered provisional measures to prevent further harm and ensure humanitarian aid access. Hearings continued into 2025, with reports from UN Special Rapporteurs documenting patterns of starvation, forced displacement, and obstruction of medical relief.

Meanwhile, mass protests erupted worldwide:

In London, over 800,000 people joined the largest Palestine solidarity march in UK history.

In New York, demonstrators filled Grand Central Station chanting *"Ceasefire Now!"*

In Amman, Cape Town, Jakarta, Paris, and São Paulo, crowds demanded an end to the siege.

In Tel Aviv, thousands of Israelis joined peace activists calling for prisoner exchanges and a permanent ceasefire.

The UN General Assembly Resolution ES-10/22 passed with 153 votes in favour, demanding an "immediate, durable, and sustained humanitarian truce."
Though vetoed repeatedly in the Security Council, the resolution became a moral compass for the global public.

What the bombs did to buildings, they also did to soil and sea. By mid-2025, the UN Environment Programme warned that 70 percent of Gaza's agricultural land was contaminated by heavy metals and unexploded ordnance. The Mediterranean shore was thick with debris; sewage systems broken, fish stocks down by 80 percent. Still, fishermen sailed. They could go only six nautical miles out under Israeli naval rules, but they went — because the sea remained the only place where the horizon was not barbed.

In Beit Lahiya, youth groups founded the project Green Hands Gaza, turning bomb craters into gardens. They filled them with soil and seedlings of mint, parsley, and tomatoes. Layla joined on weekends, printing names of the dead on small wooden markers and placing them beside each plant. "When the roots take," she said, "we will know they forgive us for living."

By August 2025, the UN estimated that only 40 percent of displaced families had returned to their neighbourhoods. Tens of thousands still sheltered in schools or temporary housing projects. UNDP's "Gaza Forward" plan employed 12 000 local workers to clear debris and recycle rubble into new cement. Omar was one of them. He called it "building from memory."

Medical missions continued. Cuban doctors arrived in July 2025, joining Egyptian and Jordanian teams. Mobile clinics treated malnutrition and burn injuries; mental-health units ran play therapy for children haunted by explosions. The International Committee of the Red Cross reported that 70 percent of Gaza's children showed signs of post-traumatic stress, yet 92 percent still attended school when possible. Resilience was quantified in attendance sheets.

The economy was barely alive. Gaza's GDP per capita had fallen below $900 according to the World Bank's October 2025 assessment, yet small markets buzzed again with the sound of barter and survival. Women's cooperatives sold hand-embroidered keffiyeh scarves and olive-wood jewellery, alongside jars of home-made soap scented with citrus and thyme, through digital corridors built by diaspora coders. Every PayPal receipt was more than a transaction — it was a message from the outside world whispering that they had not been forgotten.

And amid the rubble, weddings returned. One June evening, Layla helped organize a ceremony in a courtyard lit by solar fairy lights. The bride walked between two collapsed walls carrying a bouquet of wild anemones. When the generator failed, the guests kept singing in the dark. Someone recorded it; the video went viral under the caption: "Joy is our resistance."

By autumn 2025, news crews had moved on to other crises: Sudan's civil war, Ukraine's stalemate, the wildfires in California. But those who had seen Gaza could not forget. Documentaries aired on Arte and BBC World. In Venice, the Biennale opened its first Palestinian pavilion since 2019, featuring a photographic installation called "We Still Have Sky." In The Hague, crowds gathered outside the ICJ each hearing day with olive branches and paper kites.

Layla watched footage of those vigils on a neighbour's phone and whispered, "They remember." She looked around at her own city — half shadow, half-light — and added, "Then we must deserve their memory."

For the first time since the bombing, she felt the horizon was not locked. It moved, slowly, painfully — but it moved. And in that motion, Gaza became not just a tragedy but a mirror, forcing the world to ask what civilization means when survival itself must be rebuilt by hand.

When the guns finally quieted, silence did not sound like peace.

It sounded like the pause between breaths — the moment before the world decides whether to live or let go.

In January 2025, after months of tense negotiations in Cairo, Egypt, Jordan, and Qatar announced a fragile five-year ceasefire plan under UN supervision, later called the Cairo Framework. It promised the phased reopening of Gaza's crossings and an internationally monitored reconstruction effort. The first convoys that entered through Rafah carried sacks of wheat from Türkiye, generators from Jordan, and medical kits marked with blue UN symbols. They rolled slowly through cratered streets, greeted by children waving pieces of white cloth. For the first time in almost two years, morphine reached the hospitals, and fuel reached the incubators. The world called it a new beginning. Inside Gaza, people simply called it a breath.

From the rubble, the work of repair began. In Khan Younis, Omar joined a UNDP programme that taught local masons to press recycled rubble into new eco-bricks, each stamped with a small olive-leaf emblem — destruction turned to foundation. He kept one in his pocket as a reminder that nothing is utterly lost if it can be remade. In Rafah, Nurse Rasha reopened the maternity ward with solar panels donated by Engineers Without Borders. When the first incubator hummed again, she whispered, "This is what a ceasefire sounds like."

Layla, meanwhile, revived her women's embroidery cooperative. They stitched tatreez patterns on salvaged fabric and added QR codes linking to stories of the artisans. Each dress exported to Europe carried the tag Made in Gaza — Stitched in Hope. Buyers scanned and read Um Hassan's story from Beit Lahiya, or Amal's from Deir al-Balah. "We don't export fabric," Layla said. "We export memory."

While politicians argued over demilitarization clauses, civil society rebuilt with quiet urgency. Doctors Without Borders reopened field hospitals; World Central Kitchen fed fifty thousand people a day from container bakeries; Human Rights Watch, Amnesty International, and B'Tselem issued joint reports calling for accountability. Faith-based groups from Jakarta to Dublin launched Ramadan for Gaza campaigns that filled empty kitchens. The Palestinian Youth Forum trained hundreds of volunteers in trauma care and rubble clearance. New foreign volunteers arrived — Cuban doctors, Italian architects, a Japanese engineer who had learned Arabic online. He told Layla, half-smiling, "We rebuild because the world owes you better physics." She corrected him softly: "Better faith."

Journalists who had fled returned to reopen bureaus in half-collapsed buildings. Reuters and Al Jazeera rebuilt offices whose bullet holes they left visible as reminders. In April 2025 they held a memorial by the sea, reading aloud the names of the 138 reporters killed since 2023. Mariam filmed the ceremony for her blog. "Every camera," she wrote, "is a candle that keeps burning."

At the same time, The Hague stirred. The International Court of Justice resumed hearings on South Africa's genocide case; the International Criminal Court collected evidence of deliberate starvation and indiscriminate bombing. In one exhibit, a line from Layla's blog — We are still here — appeared in translation. Watching the clip online, she covered her mouth. "Then they heard us," she whispered.

In April, the ICC issued arrest warrants for several commanders and ministers accused of war crimes. The move divided governments but shifted the moral axis. Later that year, the UN Human Rights Council established a reparations registry for civilian victims. Bureaucracy, for once, bent toward mercy.

The next battle was environmental. UN scientists warned that Gaza's soil was poisoned with heavy metals and explosives, its aquifers brackish, its sea lined with wreckage. Out of that warning grew the Olive Tree Initiative — an alliance of local farmers, agronomists, and faith groups that planted a hundred thousand saplings across the Strip. Each was geotagged so donors abroad could "adopt" a tree. Omar planted one beside their rebuilt home and named it Sabreen — Patience. When the first leaves unfurled, Mariam traced them in her notebook, shading the green as if colour itself were fragile.

Art, too, returned. The Dar Qandeel Theatre reopened under a canvas roof, staging a play about a girl who grows a garden inside a ruined house. In Khan Younis, a poetry festival recited verses by Heba Abu Nada and Mahmoud Darwish; graffiti artists painted whole façades with the line on this earth, what makes life worth living.

A European critic called Gaza "the new post-war Florence."

"Florence had patrons," Layla replied. "We have courage."

Beyond Gaza, the moral reckoning reached parliaments and pulpits. In London, lawmakers voted to suspend export licences for weapons "potentially usable in Gaza." In Washington, protests swelled during the 2025 election year, forcing candidates to speak the word ceasefire aloud. South Africa's Constitutional Court cited its ICJ case as precedent for humanitarian litigation. Pope Francis dedicated his Easter homily to "the mothers of Gaza and Israel who cry the same salt tears." Even in Israeli newspapers, columnists began to discuss reconciliation; one quoted Mariam's viral sentence: Peace is not signed, it is planted.

At home, peace was lived more quietly — in the rhythm of reopened bakeries and repaired classrooms, in Rasha's infants who now survived their first birthdays, in Layla's students who learned coding instead of evacuation drills. Every act of normalcy was an act of defiance.

One evening, the family walked slowly toward the shore. The air was cool, laced with salt and the faint hum of engines from the fishing boats scattered along the horizon. For the first time in years, the navy had extended Gaza's fishing limit to twelve nautical miles — twice what it had been the year before. Omar shaded his eyes against the last light and smiled.

"Maybe next year, twenty," he said.

Mariam ran ahead, her bare feet sinking into the wet sand. She lifted her kite into the wind — its tail embroidered with her mother's words: We know how to begin. The fabric caught the sea breeze and climbed, tugging against the string until it vanished into the deepening dusk. For a long moment, they stood in silence, unable to tell where sky ended and thread began.

The world beyond Gaza was changing too — not all at once, not in miracles, but in fragments. Conscience did not come like thunder; it arrived in gestures: a protest sign raised in a foreign square, a doctor's hand reaching across borders, a line of code written to rebuild, a sapling planted where ash once lay. Small things, quiet things — yet each indispensable. The Cairo Framework for peace remained fragile, but beneath it, life multiplied in the cracks. And from a distance, under the fading sun, Gaza shimmered not like a wound, but like light.

That night, when the house fell into the soft rhythm of sleep, Layla sat by the open window, the scent of jasmine drifting in from the balcony. The moonlight spread pale and tender across the pages of her worn notebook — the same one she had carried through blackouts, bombardments, and births. The paper felt thin, almost translucent, as if it too had learned to survive by becoming lighter.

She hesitated before writing, listening to the distant echo of waves against the breakwater. Then, slowly, her pen began to move:

"There is no ending here — only breath, only continuation.

The sea still returns. The sun still rises.

We rebuild not to defy death, but to remind life that it belongs here too.

One day, Mariam will read these words and know that her city was not made of sorrow,

but of stubborn light."

She paused, then added one final line — small, almost hidden at the bottom of the page:

"If they ever ask what Gaza was, tell them — it was love that refused to die."

Layla closed the journal and traced the cover with her fingers, feeling the grooves of every letter written through years of dust and hope. Outside, the waves rolled closer, folding the night into a kind of prayer. Somewhere beyond the horizon, dawn waited — patient as forgiveness.

Part 4 — What You Can Do

When the rubble settled and the sky fell quiet, the world faced its reflection.

The question was no longer what happened in Gaza? but what will we do with what we saw?

Bearing witness is not a posture; it is a practice. It begins in the eyes and ends in the hands. In the years since the siege began, truth itself has become an endangered species. Misinformation, doctored footage, false captions — all were weapons that travelled faster than shrapnel. In 2024, one hundred and thirty-eight journalists from Gaza were killed, the deadliest year for the press since records began. Yet their videos, their live feeds through smoke and broken signal, kept the conscience of the world from going blind.

To honour them is to keep verifying. To ask, whenever you read: Where was the writer standing? With the people or above them?

Those who stood with Gaza told the story clearly. From the courtyards of Al-Zaytoun to the shelters of Rafah, reporters from Al Jazeera English, Haaretz, The Guardian, Middle East Eye, +972 Magazine, and B'Tselem carried words like stretchers. The United Nations OCHA situation reports, UNRWA updates, and dispatches from the Red Crescent became a new kind of scripture — imperfect, dry, factual, yet sacred because they kept record of survival. Reading carefully became a moral act. Sharing responsibly became an oath.

But knowledge without motion is another form of silence. So, action began, one person at a time. Donations flowed again through the verified channels: the UNRWA Gaza Emergency Appeal, Medical Aid for Palestinians, Doctors Without Borders, the World Food Programme, Save the Children, Palestine Red Crescent Society, and UNICEF. Each dollar became a grain of bread, a litre of fuel, a child's vaccine. The amounts were small

— six dollars and eighty cents to feed a child for a week — but in Gaza mathematics has never been about numbers, only endurance.

Layla used to tell her students that solidarity is measured not by distance but by attention. "If you remember our names," she said, "your help is not charity, it's partnership." She would laugh at the word donor — it sounded to her like a title from another planet. "You can't donate compassion," she said. "You can only return it."

Outside, the voices of Gaza multiplied online. In 2025, despite power cuts and blocked signals, poets and medics posted through satellite links, their faces grainy but their truth sharp. The world learned new names: Motaz Azaiza, Bisan Owda, Plestia Alaqad, Hind Khoudary. Their videos reached millions, each frame a defiance.

Mariam followed them, sharing translations on her blog. "Our stories don't need pity," she wrote. "They need Wi-Fi and the will to listen."

As governments debated, citizens began to act. Letters crossed oceans. Petitions filled inboxes of parliaments from Oslo to Ottawa. In London and Madrid, crowds demanded suspension of arms sales. In Washington, students occupied campuses, chanting for an end to complicity. By spring 2025, the United Nations Human Rights Council had created a reparations registry; the International Criminal Court issued arrest warrants for commanders accused of starvation tactics; the International Court of Justice continued its hearings on genocide.

For Layla, watching from a screen lit by solar power, these developments felt distant yet intimate. Each headline was a small window opening toward accountability. She printed one article and pinned it beside her desk: Ireland, Norway, and Spain

Recognize the State of Palestine. "Recognition," she murmured, "is another word for breathing."

Faith groups also joined. In churches, synagogues, mosques, and temples, prayers turned outward. In Jakarta, a million people fasted "for the mothers of Gaza." In Rome, the Vatican colonnades shone green and white for peace. In Tel Aviv, rabbis and imams studied the same verses on compassion, streaming their meetings under the name Abraham's Table. Pope Francis said that Easter, "The commandment Thou shalt not kill knows no border." Layla copied it into her notebook between recipes and receipts.

Memory itself became movement. The Palestinian Digital Memory Project began archiving diaries and photos; Layla's blog, Echoes of Tomorrow, joined its first collection. At Birzeit University and Columbia, students studied her words beside Darwish's. Museums opened new wings — in Berlin, in Santiago, in Cape Town — showing Gaza's photographs next to those of other struggles. On a mural in Johannesburg, someone painted her line: We know how to begin.

Meanwhile, grassroots efforts sprouted everywhere. In the United Kingdom, teachers paired their classrooms with Gaza schools, exchanging art through WhatsApp under the banner Olive Branch Classrooms. In Nairobi, students collected twenty thousand textbooks for displaced children. In Canada, a small bakery network called Bread Without Borders sent ovens rebuilt from scrap metal. Diaspora programmers launched Tech4Freedom, giving Gazan students VPNs and online courses. Each act was a filament in a growing net of care, thin but unbreakable.

Layla believed that faith in humanity must be practiced like a language: used daily, even when imperfect. She attended

201

interfaith vigils by video call, her face lit by candlelight. "Empathy," she said, "is resistance with a gentle voice."

Hope, in Gaza, was never abstract. It was logistics. By mid-2025, solar micro-grids powered two hundred thousand homes. Cooperatives produced bread, software, and bricks. Mariam ran a coding class in a container classroom, teaching children to map destroyed buildings with drones. When asked why she taught instead of leaving, she answered, "Because if they can erase our maps, we'll draw them again." Her students named their app Tamas — Connection.

What can one reader do, standing far from this shore? More than you think. Read carefully. Speak precisely. Correct falsehoods even when it costs you comfort. Refuse to let cruelty hide behind complexity. Support those who rebuild, and those who record. Organize, translate, educate. Each act may seem small — but memory is made of small, stubborn lights.

Layla's final post ended not with plea but with invitation: "If the world will not open the gates,

then we will open its heart."

Now that gate stands before every reader. To read this story and stop here would be to let the silence resume. To act, in any form, is to keep the page turning.

Outside, the sea hums as it always has. In the distance, the lights of Rafah shimmer from new solar arrays. Somewhere, a child writes her first poem under their glow. And across oceans, another child reads her words on a screen. Between them stretches the invisible bridge of witness — fragile, luminous, alive.

Part 5 — The Story That Continues

On the last page of her journal, Mariam writes: "We are not waiting for history to remember us. We are writing it."

The candle beside her flickers, its flame bending in the draft from the broken window. Outside, the sea rolls against the shore — endless, patient, and knowing. In Gaza, even the sea understands time differently. It has seen empires rise and fall, seen ships arrive with crusaders, traders, and refugees. It has carried olive wood and ashes, prayers, and debris. Now it carries silence, and the faint echo of children's laughter returning after too many seasons of fear.

Mariam closes her notebook and listens. Somewhere beyond the shoreline, a generator hums to life; somewhere else, a muezzin calls the dawn prayer. The words — Hayya 'ala al-falah — come like an answer to her own. "Come to success." Even here, after everything, the call still means something.

In a café in Ramallah, a journalist edits a feature titled "The Daughters of Gaza." The headline glows on his laptop screen, his reflection dim in the glass. The article begins with Mariam's quote, continues with Layla's story, ends with a photograph of Omar standing beside a wall he rebuilt. He adjusts the caption: Reconstruction worker, Gaza, 2025. Hope under scaffolding. When he sends it to press, he whispers, "May they see you as I do — alive."

In Paris, under the grey light of a Sunday morning, a student named Camille reads Mariam's translated blog for the first time. She is twenty-one, studying international law, sipping coffee in a small apartment near the Seine. Each post opens like a wound and closes like a prayer. When she reaches the one titled The Sea Between Us, she stops, hand over her mouth. "We are not waiting for history…" she reads aloud. And suddenly, Gaza feels near — not as a headline, but as a heartbeat. That afternoon, she joins a group painting a mural on the university wall: a girl flying a kite above broken house. Underneath, she writes in French, "Nous écrivons l'histoire." We are writing history.

In Nairobi, the morning sun falls through the classroom windows of Kawangware Primary. Children crouch over sheets of paper, drawing kites labelled Peace, Love, Home. Their teacher, who once volunteered in a UN refugee program, tells them about Gaza. "They build even when the world forgets them," she says. The children ask if they can send their drawings. She smiles. "One day, you will."

Meanwhile, in Cape Town, a choir rehearses for a concert to raise funds for Gaza reconstruction. Their voices rise through the rafters: a mix of Xhosa, Arabic, and English. Salaam, shalom, peace. Across the ocean in Buenos Aires, a street artist paints an olive tree sprouting from a pile of rubble, its roots wrapping around the planet. He tags it #GazaLives.

History, once indifferent, begins to turn — slowly, painfully, but unmistakably. It turns in courtrooms where lawyers argue for accountability; in parliaments where resolutions are debated; in refugee camps where doctors rebuild from dust. It turns in classrooms, cafés, protests, and prayers. The pivot is not made by generals or presidents but by ordinary people who refuse to look away. The world, long fractured by apathy, rediscovers its pulse in the faces of those who survived.

In 2025, the rebuilding continues. The UN records show that 70 percent of Gaza's rubble has been cleared. Solar panels bloom across the rooftops like metallic sunflowers. Reopened schools teach a new curriculum that includes lessons on trauma and environmental recovery. The olive tree initiative has planted 100,000 saplings, each one tagged with GPS coordinates so its caretaker abroad can watch it grow. The trees are thriving. "It's as if the soil forgives faster than we do," Omar says.

Layla's cooperative has reopened full-time. Their embroidered dresses appear in a fashion show in Milan under the title Threads of Survival. Each gown tells a story stitched in tatreez — a symbol for village, a line for the wall, a circle for the sea. The audience stands in silence as the models walk the runway barefoot, carrying candles. When the lights dim, Layla's recorded voice plays: "We do not make clothes. We make continuations."

Rasha, the nurse, runs a clinic now powered entirely by solar energy. She delivers babies in rooms lit by sunlight instead of diesel fumes. One afternoon she holds a newborn in her arms and whispers, "You were born free of the sound of drones." The mother, exhausted but smiling, asks her the baby's weight. Rasha looks at the scale and says, "Three kilograms of tomorrow."

During rebuilding, grief and joy coexist. Many families are still missing, their names now memorialised on walls. Yet even these walls bloom with colour. Artists paint vines, doves, and verses of hope. Children add handprints in bright red and yellow. Every print says the same thing: We were here.

Far away, the world's great powers continue to argue. The International Court of Justice prepares its final judgment. The Security Council debates sanctions and aid packages. Analysts write columns about "the Gaza precedent." But on the ground, none of those words can rebuild a kitchen or comfort a child. What rebuilds is touch, patience, and repetition — the quiet rhythm of people who decide to stay.

On Fridays, the markets of Gaza City pulse again with life. The air smells of sumac and frying bread. Fishermen sell sardines fresh from the sea. A street musician plays an oud repaired with fishing wire, singing Darwish's lines: "We have on this earth what makes life worth living." Shoppers hum along while haggling for cucumbers. The smallness of these moments is their victory.

In the evenings, Layla walks with Omar and Mariam along the shore. They watch the horizon where the sea meets the fading sky, the line between captivity and infinity. "Do you think the world will change?" Mariam asks.

Omar looks at the water, always moving yet always returning to the same sand. "It already has," he says. "It's remembering."

That night, Mariam writes again in her journal. She adds to her final entry: "History doesn't remember us. We are history remembering itself."

The candle burns low. Layla closes the window against the salt wind. The city beyond them glows with solar lights, each rooftop a small constellation. Somewhere beyond the border, protests continue; in Washington, another resolution is debated; in Cape Town, a new mural is painted. The world moves — awkwardly, haltingly, but it moves.

When the flame finally dies, its smoke curls upward like a thread connecting all those who refused to stop believing. In that darkened room, Gaza feels like the centre of something vast — not only pain, but possibility.

Outside, the waves keep time. Somewhere, a baby is born. Somewhere, a pen is lifted. Somewhere, a protestor lights a candle and chants the word, Freedom. And in the rhythm of these acts — small, stubborn, luminous — the world rediscovers itself.

Today, Gaza stands as both a tragedy and a testimony. Every generation here learns two languages — the language of survival and the language of hope. From ancient empires to modern sieges, the story of Gaza has never been about surrender. It is a history of people who refuse to disappear.

Each evening, as the sun falls into the Mediterranean, the city's minarets and church towers echo together in the same fading light. Fishermen still sail into waters marked by danger. Mothers still tell their children, "Tomorrow will be better."

And, one day, it will. Because every stone in Gaza, every surviving wall, every child who dares to dream is proof that remembrance is stronger than ruin — and that even in a land scarred by centuries, life continues to rise from the dust.

1.14 ACKNOWLEDGEMENTS

This book was written in honour of the people of Gaza — the mothers who rebuild from dust and memory, the fathers who continue to teach with patience even when classrooms have no walls, and the children who still dream beyond fences. It is dedicated to every heartbeat that endured, to every story that refused to disappear, and to every act of tenderness that survived the noise of war. It exists because of those who chose hope over despair, and creation over silence.

My deepest gratitude goes to the journalists and photographers who risked their lives to bear witness. You carried cameras through smoke and rubble, wrote your dispatches by the light of burning candles, and turned your witness into the conscience of the world. Because of you, truth did not vanish in the dark. Your courage is the living archive of our time.

To the medics and humanitarian workers who stood between life and loss — the nurses who pumped air by hand when generators failed, the doctors and paramedics who ran toward danger instead of away from it, and the volunteers who shared their food with strangers before feeding themselves — your compassion redrew the boundaries of what it means to be human. You gave meaning to service, and dignity to suffering.

To the educators, poets, and artists whose work kept Gaza human — the teachers who drew letters on torn cardboard when there were no books, the painters who transformed rubble into colour, the musicians who found a way to make harmony in a city of sirens — your creativity and courage have been the breath of this place. You reminded the world that art is not a luxury; it is proof of life.

To the readers, advocates, and witnesses around the world who refused to look away — those who marched in cities far from the sea, who raised flags, wrote letters, and kept speaking when silence felt easier — your solidarity was a light crossing border. Every act of empathy, every post, every prayer, every protest carried the message that Gaza was not forgotten.

To the countless unnamed people whose strength often went unrecorded — the neighbours who shared bread, the children who planted olive saplings in dust, and the women who mended both clothes and hearts — your quiet perseverance became the foundation of every page in this book. Without your daily acts of kindness and endurance, there would be no story to tell.

To the memory of those who did not survive, may your names become roots in every story yet to be told. May your laughter fill the halls once restored, and may the world eventually become kind enough to be worthy of remembering you. To those who live, may your light outlast the dark. May your hands rebuild what was broken, may your voices fill the silence, and may your dreams always reach farther than the fences that surround you.

This book belongs to you. It was written for you. You are the proof that even in the deepest night, humanity still endures — fragile, luminous, and fiercely alive.

1.15 ABBREVIATION LIST

A.D. — Anno Domini

BCE — Before Common Era

CARE — Cooperative for Assistance and Relief Everywhere

CE — Common Era

COVID-19 — Coronavirus Disease 2019

EU — European Union

FAO — Food and Agriculture Organization (of the United Nations)

GDP — Gross Domestic Product

IDF — Israel Defence Forces

ILO — International Labour Organization

NGO — Non-Governmental Organization

NGOs — Non-Governmental Organizations

OCHA — Office for the Coordination of Humanitarian Affairs (United Nations)

Oxfam — Oxford Committee for Famine Relief

PA — Palestinian Authority

PCBS — Palestinian Central Bureau of Statistics

PLO — Palestine Liberation Organization

UN — United Nations

UNDP — United Nations Development Programme

UNESCO — United Nations Educational, Scientific and Cultural Organization

UNGA — United Nations General Assembly

UNHCR — United Nations High Commissioner for Refugees

UNICEF — United Nations International Children's Emergency Fund

UNRWA — United Nations Relief and Works Agency for Palestine Refugees in the Near East

UNSC — United Nations Security Council

UN Women — United Nations Entity for Gender Equality and the Empowerment of Women

WFP — World Food Programme

WHO — World Health Organization

WB — World Bank

1.16 REFERENCES AND SOURCES

United Nations & International Institutions

- UN OCHA: *Occupied Palestinian Territory Humanitarian Update* (2023–2025)

- UN General Assembly Resolution ES-10/22 (Dec 12, 2024)

- UN Security Council Briefings (Jan–June 2025)

- ICJ Case: *South Africa v. Israel* (Provisional Measures Orders, 2024–2025)

- WHO Situation Reports, Gaza Health Cluster (2024–2025)

- UNRWA Gaza Emergency Situation Reports (2023–2025) Human Rights & Legal

- Amnesty International: *Israel/OPT: Evidence of War Crimes in Gaza* (2024)

211

- Human Rights Watch: *Starvation Used as a Weapon of War* (2024)

- B'Tselem: *Conquer and Destroy — Israeli Policy in Gaza* (2025)

- International Criminal Court filings: *Situation in Palestine* (ongoing) Journalism & Analysis

- Al Jazeera English Gaza War Coverage (2023–2025)

- The Guardian Investigations: *Inside Gaza's Siege* (2024)

- Haaretz: *The Cost of the War* (2024–2025)

- +972 Magazine: *Witnessing Gaza* Series (2024)

- The New York Times & Reuters Fact Reports (2024–2025) Civil Society & Aid Organizations

- Doctors Without Borders (MSF) – Field Reports 2024–2025

- Medical Aid for Palestinians (MAP) – Annual Briefs 2024

- World Central Kitchen – Gaza Relief Operations 2024–2025

- Save the Children – *Trapped Childhoods* Report (2024)

- Palestine Red Crescent Society – Situation Updates (2023–2025)

Art & Culture

- *Voices of Gaza* Anthology (Dar al-Adab, 2023)

- Mahmoud Darwish, *We Love Life Whenever We Can*

- Refaat Alareer (1979–2023), *If I Must Die*

- Local collectives: *Green Hands Gaza*, *Artists for Survival*

United Nations Relief and Works Agency for Palestine Refugees in the Near East (UNRWA).
Annual Operational Report: Gaza Strip 2023. Amman: UNRWA Publications, 2024.
https://www.unrwa.org/resources/reports

United Nations Office for the Coordination of Humanitarian Affairs (OCHA).
Gaza Strip Humanitarian Snapshot – December 2024. Jerusalem: OCHA Occupied Palestinian Territory, 2024.
https://www.ochaopt.org

World Health Organization (WHO).
Right to Health: Barriers to Medical Access in the Gaza Strip, 2024. Geneva: WHO Eastern Mediterranean Regional Office, 2024.
https://www.emro.who.int

United Nations Educational, Scientific and Cultural Organization (UNESCO).
Education in Gaza: Resilience Through Learning, 2023. Paris: UNESCO, 2023. https://www.unesco.org

United Nations Development Programme (UNDP).
Microenterprise Support in Gaza – Women's Cooperatives and Livelihoods Report, 2022. New York: UNDP Regional Bureau for Arab States, 2022. https://www.undp.org

We Are Not Numbers (WANN).
Voices of Gaza Anthology. Gaza City: We Are Not Numbers Project, 2023.
https://wearenotnumbers.org

Save the Children International.
The Hidden Trauma: The Mental Health Crisis Among Gaza's Youth, 2023. London: Save the Children, 2023.
https://www.savethechildren.net

Palestinian Central Bureau of Statistics (PCBS).
Household Survey on Labour Force and Living Conditions in the Gaza Strip, 2022. Ramallah: PCBS, 2023.
https://pcbs.gov.ps

UNICEF.
State of Palestine: Children under Blockade – Annual Humanitarian Report 2023. New York: UNICEF, 2024.
https://www.unicef.org

World Food Programme (WFP).
Food Security Assessment: Gaza Strip 2023. Rome: WFP, 2023.
https://www.wfp.org

Amnesty International.
Israel/OPT: The Gaza Blockade – Collective Punishment in Violation of International Law, 2024. London: Amnesty International, 2024. https://www.amnesty.org

Human Rights Watch (HRW).
Gaza: Fifteen Years of Blockade – Lives Trapped, Futures Denied, 2023. New York: HRW, 2023. https://www.hrw.org

International Committee of the Red Cross (ICRC).
Gaza under Fire: Health, Water, and Humanitarian Access, 2023. Geneva: ICRC, 2023. https://www.icrc.org

Médecins Sans Frontières (MSF).
Field Notes from Gaza: Mental Health and Emergency Medicine Reports, 2022–2024. Paris: MSF, 2024. https://www.msf.org

United Nations Human Rights Council (UNHRC).
Report of the Independent International Commission of Inquiry on the Occupied Palestinian Territory, Including East Jerusalem, and Israel, 2024. Geneva: United Nations, 2024. https://www.ohchr.org

"They tried to bury us.
They didn't know we were seeds."

From the olive trees to the sea, from rubble to classroom,

from memory to page —

Gaza lives.
And so does love.

www.ingramcontent.com/pod-product-compliance
Lightning Source LLC
Chambersburg PA
CBHW071337090426
42738CB00012B/2921